Comics

Comics: An Introduction provides a clear and detailed introduction to the Comics form – including graphic narratives and a range of other genres – explaining key terms, history, theories, and major themes. The book uses a variety of examples to show the rich history as well as the current cultural relevance and significance of Comics.

Taking a broadly global approach, Harriet Earle discusses the history and development of the form internationally, as well as how to navigate comics as a new way of reading. Earle also pushes beyond the book to lay out the ways that fans engage with their comics of choice – and how this can impact the industry. She also analyses how Comics can work for social change and political comment. Discussing journalism and life writing, she examines how the coming together of word and image gives us new ways to discuss our world and ourselves.

A glossary and further reading section help those new to Comics solidify their understanding and further their exploration of this dynamic and growing field.

Harriet E.H. Earle is Lecturer in English at Sheffield Hallam University, UK. Her first monograph – *Comics, Trauma, and the New Art of War* – was published in 2017. Her research interests include American Comics and popular culture, representations of violence, protest narratives, and biopolitics. She has published across the field of Comics and popular culture studies. She is also the Editor of the series *Global Perspectives in Comics Studies*.

Comics

An Introduction

Harriet E.H. Earle

Routledge
Taylor & Francis Group

LONDON AND NEW YORK

First published 2021
by Routledge
2 Park Square, Milton Park, Abingdon, Oxon OX14 4RN

and by Routledge
52 Vanderbilt Avenue, New York, NY 10017

Routledge is an imprint of the Taylor & Francis Group, an informa business

British Library Cataloguing-in-Publication Data
A catalogue record for this book is available from the British Library

Library of Congress Cataloging-in-Publication Data
Names: Earle, Harriet E.H., author.
Title: Comics: an introduction / Harriet E.H. Earle.
Description: Abingdon, Oxon; New York, NY: Routledge, 2021. |
Includes bibliographical references and index.
Identifiers: LCCN 2020033300 | ISBN 9780367322410 (paperback) |
ISBN 9780367322427 (hardback) | ISBN 9780429317484 (ebook)
Subjects: LCSH: Comic books, strips, etc.–History and criticism. |
Graphic novels–History and criticism.
Classification: LCC PN6710 .E27 2021 | DDC 741.5/9–dc23
LC record available at https://lccn.loc.gov/2020033300

ISBN: 978-0-367-32242-7 (hbk)
ISBN: 978-0-367-32241-0 (pbk)
ISBN: 978-0-429-31748-4 (ebk)

Typeset in Bembo
by Newgen Publishing UK

For Dr Fuhs, my very own Jolly Jumper

Contents

Figures

Acknowledgements

This is my favourite part of the book to write – an outpouring of gratitude to everyone who made it happen.

Thank you to the team at Routledge who brought this book into being: Polly Dodson, Zoe Meyer, and all those who worked 'behind the scenes' to bring this book to life. To Professor Chris Hopkins and Richard Wood for preparing my index.

The beautiful diagrams in Chapter 1 are the work of Rozi Hathaway and Sam Williams – thank you for your fantastic work! Thank you to everyone who gave me permission to use their images: Hannah Berry, Joe Sacco, Tom Gauld, Pascal Jousselin, Jeph Jacques, Una, Dr Ian Williams, Dr John Miers, and Dr Nicola Streeten. Special thanks to Kaitlyn Gilman for her cosplay photo and to Tom Price for (patiently) showing me how to make infographics.

Thank you to the staff at Sheffield Hallam University Library, University of Sheffield Library, the John Rylands Library, and Sheffield Central Library for giving me a space to work and, often, help with finding stuff.

To Dr Laurike In T' Veld and Dr Eszter Szép – the Glamorous Ladies of Comics and my dear friends – for proofreading, listening, and discussing. To Dr Sasha Garwood-Lloyd, for her friendship and reliable stream of feminist commentary and kickassery. To Dr Donna Cox, for her age-old wisdom. To Joanna Dobson, whose proofreading skills are formidable and brilliant, as she is. And Steven Burke, who gives excellent advice. And Erin Burrell, my favourite collaborator.

Uncontained gratitude to my wonderful and supportive Comics comrades. I am indebted to all of you for your friendship, support, suggestions, and, of course, dog pictures.

Dr Martin Lund, Dr Sarah Lightman, Dr Johannes Schmid, Alex Fitch, Dr Lise Tannahill, Felix Kühn Ravn, Dr Fernanda Basteris, Dr Christina Meyer, Dr Mihaela Precup, Dr Paul Fisher Davies, Charlotte Fabricius, Barbara Chamberlin, Dr Joachim Trinkwitz, Dr Paul Williams, Dr Simon Grennan, Dr Judith Muskett, Harry Taylor, Kathy Davis, Joe Stanley, Hannah Bayley, Chris Sykes, Dr Jotham Gaudoin, Isabella Earle, and Matilda Earle.

And, thank you to Carsten, who read this book at least four times over and still has good things to say about it. There aren't enough thanks in the world for your love, support, and declensions.

Introduction

Comics: no laughing matter

Most people have read a comic without knowing they are doing so. Comic books are part of the reading diets of people of all nationalities, ages, genders, and educational levels. Even for those who have not consciously picked up a comic book, the same basic form and ways of communication of information can be found in a large number of documents that are common in our modern world, from the instructions for flat pack furniture or flight safety leaflets, to viral memes posted on social media platforms. These are not strictly Comics, as I will show, but they are narratives told primarily via images, positioned in sequence, and, at their heart, this is all a comic is. The narrative of a flat pack bookcase is an easy one to decipher – 'do this and you'll get the finished object'. Flight safety should be easily understandable across multiple languages and educational levels, while memes tap into communal knowledge and narratives to repackage social mores and cultural truths into easily disseminated, humorous formats.

These examples are *not* Comics. But they use many of the same formal and narrative techniques as those used in Comics to convey information, to persuade, and to entertain. But if these things are not Comics, then what is? First, Comics is not picture books; it is not illustrated stories, where the images are supplementary to understanding the written text. Let us consider a famous definition of Comics, from Scott McCloud's 1994 book *Understanding Comics*. He writes that 'Comics is [*sic*] juxtaposed pictorial and other images in a deliberate sequence, intended to convey information and/or produce an aesthetic response in the viewer' (1994: 9). This definition is comprehensive, but the necessary keywords are in the first part – 'juxtaposed [...] in deliberate sequence'. For McCloud, Comics places images in specific sequences in order to tell a story, and his focus is on the primacy of the image. Comics creator and editor Will Eisner is more succinct in his definition: for him, the Comics form is 'sequential art' (2008a). It is imperative that we keep this idea at the forefront of our minds, for it is central to the essence of Comics.

In Chapter 1, I discuss in detail the term 'Comics', its uses, and the many specific categories that fall under it. It is used in two ways: both as an abstract and a concrete noun. 'Comics', with a capital letter and used in the singular, is the abstract, and is used to refer to the form itself; it is also used this way to discuss the industry. With a lower-case letter, it is a concrete noun, to refer to the material (or digital) 'thing' – a comic book or some comics, for example. Though the distinction is slight, this allows the form and the material object to remain distinct in discussion.

Comics demands images to be placed in sequence and, furthermore, demands a readership that can negotiate these images in order to create a coherent narrative that will engage the reader. This is a concern that exists across the entire spectrum of Comics, from the shortest newspaper strip (such as *Garfield* by Jim Davis [1978–present] or *Peanuts* by Charles Schulz [1950–2000]) to epic multi-volume series (e.g., *Cerebus* by Dave Sim [1977–2004] or *Saga* by Brian K. Vaughan and Fiona Staples [2012–present]). In his 1964 book *Understanding Media: The Extensions of Man*, philosopher Marshall McLuhan coined the now-famous phrase, 'the medium is the message'. The way that a piece of media (be it a piece of text, a comic, or any other type) is produced and represented is as important as what it says; its form can determine meaning and reception. As this book will demonstrate, Comics is all about the form in a way that is distinct from other narrative media, and the reader is an active participant in the creation of the story simply by the way they choose to read and make connections between the images on the page. Not only does the reader have to navigate the reading and understanding of both text and image, but they are also expected to navigate the layout of the page – and the whole comic – themselves. This involves making choices about the path to take through the images, the speed at which to read each image and the types of connections that can be made between image and image, as well as word and image.

Until relatively recently, the study of Comics has been sitting on the sidelines of the academy, despite the popularity of the form and its ubiquity within popular culture. Comics is one of the oldest and most dynamic narrative forms on the planet, one that makes complex stories accessible and understandable for a diverse, international readership. Many scholars and creators have suggested alternative terms that overcome the misconceptions associated with the name, as I discuss in Chapter 1, but none has stuck. Within universities, Comics Studies is highly inter-disciplinary; scholars from various departments such as English, History, Psychology, Graphic Design, Art, and Media Studies do research on it. The subject has not yet been 'consecrated by the academy', to use Pierre Bourdieu's term (1991), and so is not technically a discipline. This raises all kinds of questions; the mobile nature of researchers across various disciplines enriches scholarship by interaction. Not being a discipline gives Comics Studies the freedom of not being strictly 'disciplined'; scholar-ship is not bound by certain discourses and patterns of know-ledge that others face. However, it also means that it is largely homeless, and this comes with a lack of belonging and collective resources that lead to questions of legitimacy and impact. In Figure I.1, Comics scholar Roger Sabin (here drawn as Snoopy from Schulz' *Peanuts* strips) suggests two potential advantages to Comics Studies becoming a discipline. Because Comics Studies is an interdisciplinary field, it brings together cognate disciplines; when they interact with each other they share and expand the arsenal of analytical tools. This is to the benefit of the field and allows for a rich diversity of analytical approaches, as well as offers a nexus for disciplines to come together on common ground for the discussion and interrogation of a particular topic or theme. It is important to understand the context in which this field is situated, as it has a massive bearing on how Comics is viewed both within universities and in wider society. It also helps to see

Figure I.1 Roger Sabin as Schulz's 'Snoopy' by John Miers (2019).

where the scholarship is rooted and how it is being constructed in relation to existing modes of knowledge and analytical methods.

This introduction will set out some key issues for Comics and provide some short definitions, as well as signposting to later chapters in the book.

Comics is not a genre but a form all its own

In 2018, Nick Drnaso's *Sabrina* became the first comic to be longlisted for the Booker Prize, an award open to Anglophone fiction. *Sabrina* is a graphic novel (a genre of Comics that we will discuss in more detail in Chapter 1) that follows the disappearance of a young woman; the story focuses on the aftermath and its effect on her friends, the titular Sabrina does not feature prominently as a character. Though it did not reach the shortlist, Drnaso was lauded in the international press. The process of longlisting raises, in this instance, a number of key issues that involve the status of graphic novels in our culture. The Booker Prize is a *literary* award; it is designed to be given to works of literature. *Sabrina* is a graphic novel, coming under the umbrella of Comics. If it can be considered for a literary award, then so can the latest film by Quentin Tarantino or television series by Julian Fellowes.

There is much debate around the term 'graphic novel' in relation to Comics, with some scholars and creators using it interchangeably and others shunning it completely. There is a middle ground, in which we can situate 'graphic novels' as a subset of the form: all graphic novels are comics but not all comics are graphic novels. It is a type of comic book with its own nuanced history and execution, which exists in dialogue with other subsets and without hierarchy. Furthermore, Comics is a separate form; just like film, literature, or television, it exists in a cultural and publishing space that is unique and not a subset of another form. It is often said (commonly in the mass media) that Comics is a genre of literature, but this is simply not the case. On the surface of it, the connections are clear to see. Literature and Comics are both ways of telling stories that are typically read in bound books: Comics, Film, and Television are all visual forms. Though there is a large amount of crossover media now flooding the market, especially given the huge popularity of the Marvel and DC Cinematic Universes, not to mention other comics adaptations such as *The Crow* (1994), *300* (2007), and *Kingsman* (2015), these forms remain distinct. In Chapter 1, I discuss a range of basic definitions in order to reveal the nuances of different types of comics, including graphic novels, web comics, and strips. I also look at the various parts of the form itself: what are the constituent parts of the form called and how do they fit together?

Comics has a 'chequered' history

Naming the first comic is not an easy task because there is no clear beginning or foundational text. There are several ways to approach this. Many Comics histories return to prehistory, when humans first used sequential art in the form of cave paintings and petroglyphs. Others may prefer to refer to the use of recognisable elements of the form as benchmarks: for example, we may look to the first use of panels to divide and separate the art into clearly demarked images (which is attributed to the nineteenth-century schoolmaster Rodolphe Töpffer) or the inclusion of speech bubbles (which can be dated back to the use of the 'phylactery' in medieval art – see Figure I.2). Moving forward, some consider the publication location and dissemination method to be a central factor and so consider the first comic to be the first one sold in newsstands (the first to be sold in this way is *The Glasgow Looking-Glass* [1826]). There are a number of contenders for 'first comic' and all have their merits based on both formal and thematic concerns. My aim in Chapter 2 is to proceed via an examination of the earliest examples of image-driven stories that

Figure I.2 'Der Liebeszauber' by a Lower Rhine Master of the fifteenth century (c. 1470), bpk/Museum der bildenden Künste, Leipzig/Michael Ehritt.

are hidden in the depths of prehistoric caves, through several thousand years of pictures on walls, on windows, and on paper, to the modern era, when the comic as we now know it came into existence. Comics developed gradually out of a range of existing storytelling practices and techniques and its genesis was slow and meandering.

Comics is an international form

There is not a society or culture on the planet that has not developed its own type and style of Comics. Though in some countries the form is more prevalent than in others, the fact remains that comics are ubiquitous. This is true both of comics and of 'proto-comics' (a distinction that we will discuss in more detail in Chapter 2). In the case of Comics, it is not simply that the West has disseminated the form into other parts of the world as a sort of cultural colonialism, but that this form truly has developed internationally; this discussion forms part of Chapter 3. Of course, it is important to remember that the advent of the internet and the increased internationalisation of publishing strategies affect what gets published, how, and where, an issue that we will develop through this chapter. It follows on from an Anglophone history in Chapter 2, broadens the geographic scope of the form to consider in more detail the ways in which Comics has become an international form. With special focus on *Manga* (Japanese) and *Bandes Dessinées* (Franco-Belgian), as well as Italian, Spanish, Indian, and Korean comics, this chapter will seek to show the different international contexts in which Comics developed and the current understanding of the form in other countries. For example, the Japanese Comics tradition (typically called '*Manga*') can trace roots back to scrolls from the twelfth and thirteenth centuries. In addition, several key works cemented the artistic practices of *Manga* as central to Japanese visual and narrative art, including *Tōba Ehon*, a collection of drawings from the twelfth century and the sketchbooks of Hokusai (1760–1849), perhaps more famous as a central figure in the style known as *Ukiyo-e* (Pictures of the floating world). *Manga* in the modern sense has been in use since 1900, with the launch of *Jiji Manga*, the Sunday comics page of the popular daily newspaper *Jiji Shimpo*. Though Anglophone bookshops often provide a small offering of international comics in translation, this is not truly representative since what is not translated remains inaccessible to many readers. I discuss how translation works in a visual form, and how it does not. To what extent is comics translation dependent on readerly understanding of visual signs that are socially, linguistically, or culturally specific? And what effect does this have on the comic itself?

Comics is not just about the text

The community that surrounds Comics as a cultural phenomenon is huge, with a correspondingly large number of annual conventions, dedicated collectors, and enthusiastic web fora. The fan communities exist alongside the form itself; they are something that has grown up as a parallel movement, influenced by it, and, in more recent years, exerting a reciprocal effect on it. These communities can be venues for rich, vibrant discussion but they can also become toxic. Chapter 4 will discuss the materiality of Comics with a history that is bound up with processes of production and publication, audience, fandom, and readership in a way that is unique to it as a form. The wider culture beyond the material phenomenon itself is part of the development of the comic book as 'artefact'. 'Nerd' or 'Geek culture', so called, does not begin and end with the comic book shop but encapsulates conventions and online fan communities, as well as fan production of artefacts (including artwork and fan fiction) and engagement with the creative process itself. Chapter 4 will outline some of the key issues in the culture of Comics as a wider phenomenon, what it means for both creator and consumer, and how these issues relate to the study of comics as cultural artefacts. I will also briefly discuss 'Comicsgate', a sustained campaign of online abuse and harassment against female artists, precipitated by what some perceived as 'forced diversity' in mainstream publications and what this means in terms of fan engagement and perceived 'ownership'.

Comics is for everyone

When Hannah Berry took over as the UK's Comics Laureate in 2019, she declared that 'with the enormous, diverse wealth of subjects out there, there's a comic for everybody' (BBC, 2018: n.p.). Comics span creators and characters from all demographic groups; small press and web publishing outlets remove constrictions on form or theme that may disqualify certain creators from approaching larger publishers. As with all other forms, Comics publications are targeted at a wide range of audiences. For example, long-running British comics *The Beano* (1938–present) and *The Dandy* (1937–2013) are primarily aimed at a young readership, though many continue to read them long after they leave the 'target age group'. Conversely, Neil Gaiman's multi-award-winning series *The Sandman* (1989–present) is aimed at an adult readership and includes many plot elements that are unsuitable for children. That said, Gaiman is one of a large group of comics creators who work across several age ranges. In terms of target readership, Comics is as diverse as any other form.

Unfortunately, despite a demonstrable diversity of readership and a large number of nuanced, technically accomplished texts by female and non-binary creators, some areas of Comics remain a largely male creative space. There are many long-running debates regarding the position of female and LGBT+ characters and creators within Comics. One such issue that is prominent in American comic books is the so-called 'Women in Refrigerators' trope. Named in the title of a website, created in 1999 by American writer Gail Simone, the term refers to an event in DC's *Green Lantern* #54 (1994). Superhero Kyle Rayner returns home to find his girlfriend, Alex DeWitt, had been murdered and her disarticulated body is in the refrigerator. The website consists of a list of female characters that have been raped, tortured, and/or murdered; it consists of 120 names. Simone's list clearly demonstrates that the phenomenon of violence against women is an enduring theme in comics. The list is prefaced with the following note:

> Not every woman in comics has been killed, raped, depowered, crippled, turned evil, maimed, tortured, contracted a disease or had other life-derailing tragedies befall her, but given the following list (originally compiled by Gail, with later additions and changes), it's hard to think up exceptions.
>
> (Simone, 1999: n.p.)

The point is humorously made: women's value in superhero comics is found in their position as catalyst for male action, rather than for anything to do with their own agency. The 'Women in Refrigerators' trope is often dismissed as lazy writing. The death or suffering of a female character as a catalyst for male characters devalues both characters. Storylines become expressions of simple anger and revenge, rather than ones tackling more complex themes and give a voice to female survivors of violence. Despite this criticism, the trope is rife in mainstream comics. It fundamentally devalues the place of women in Comics; the artistic milieu that it creates is hostile. Though this particular example is Amerocentric and not necessarily indicative of the state of the industry internationally, many noted Comics scholars, including Hillary Chute and Jane Tolmie, suggest that Comics *is* inherently androcentric and that this focus alienates women and non-binary artists. It is certainly true that there is a striking gender disparity in the demographics of both creators and represented characters in most types of comics; the exception to this is *Manga* (see Chapter 3). The rise of alternative and independent comics, and especially web comics, has created a space in which female and LGBT+ creators are able to make and tell the stories that speak to their experience of the world (see Chapter 2).

Comics can be world changing and life defining

Comics can – and do – change the world. This may be seen as an exaggeration, but there are two clear examples of comics that have proved to be tools for change, though we may argue that neither is positive. In 2005, the Danish newspaper *Jyllands-Posten* sparked an international controversy by publishing a series of images of the Muslim prophet Muhammad and, in January 2015, the office of the French weekly comic *Charlie Hebdo* was targeted by gunmen, provoked by the publisher's irreverent representation of Muhammad. Despite these negative examples, it is clear that Comics can mobilise people in ways that other forms have failed to do. The history of Comics as a journalistic device is long and derives from political cartooning. Chapter 5 will discuss Comics as an established form for socio-political comment, and for longer journalistic narratives, as well as a conduit for controversy. Focussing on the works of Joe Sacco, Sarah Glidden, and Guy Delisle, as well as the significant amount of editorial and political comics that appear daily in print news media and publications such as *The Nib*, I discuss the inherent issues with making socio-political comments in a visual format. I also discuss Comics as a form for social change that is both very successful and that has a rich history.

It would be short-sighted to think that Comics speaks truths only about the world *around* us; it can do the same for the intricate worlds *within* us too. A large number of comics autobiographies have been published over the past few decades, many of which deal with trauma, complex life experiences, and medical diagnoses. These (auto)biographical texts are vehicles for the representation of intensely personal and individual stories and experiences. Of course, with any kind of life writing, we face issues of representation, 'autobiographical truth', and narration, and, in some cases, of total fabrication. In her 2002 work *One! Hundred! Demons!*, Lynda Barry uses the term 'autobiofictionalography', a portmanteau term that acknowledges the amalgamation of truth and fiction that is central to life writing. The study of 'autographics' (as they are often rendered) is among the most dynamic of all areas of Comics Studies. In Chapter 6, I explore this complex area with reference to the work of Nicola Streeten (2007), Una (2015), and Nora Krug (2018); I discuss the creation of the visual 'author avatar' and suggest several reasons how and why Comics has become so successful and popular as a form of life writing.

1   Definitions and mechanics

What is Comics? What are Comics?

One common problem with a relatively new field of study and critical inquiry is that it is important to consider critically the terms used to define it. Issues of form are not yet stable, and it is, therefore, important to define the terms that are used throughout this book. The question of definitions and terminologies is one of the most hotly contested issues in what has come to be called Comics Studies. What *do* we call the form? This prompts two important and related questions: why have certain terms been used to describe this field of study? And what is the difference between, for example, comics and graphic novels? The shorthand answer is that Comics is primarily a visual form that encompasses a very broad range of genres and styles, for audiences of all ages; originally short in length, the form has expanded to include long-form narratives and to appeal to a far wider audience. What this chapter aims to do is to give a clear overview of the various terms in common use, their meaning, history, and nuance.

The term 'Comics' comes with much cultural and intellectual baggage. 'Cultural baggage' is the set of subconscious assumptions and behaviours that one may hold about a certain issue or topic, often without being aware; this baggage can affect the way we view a particular type of media. For Comics, the assumption that it is a form strictly for children or of 'low value' is an example of such baggage. Not only do these beliefs often necessitate a disclaimer at the outset of discussions, especially academic ones, to show that they are not representative of the form as a whole, but they are also often used as a way of derailing debates or discrediting the form. Comics has been an important part of cultural and literary studies debates since the 1980s and is now firmly established within contemporary scholarship.

The term comes with a grammatical quirk that requires explanation. When 'Comics' is used in relation to the form itself, it is a singular noun, as with terms such as 'Politics' or 'Ethics'; in such cases it is also usually capitalised. We can also use 'Comics' in this way when discussing the industry, retail networks, and associated institutions; it is an abstract noun as we will see in Chapter 4. Alternatively, when discussing individual texts, we use 'comics' as a plural noun, with a lower-case 'c', as in, for example, 'a comic' or 'some comics'. Here it is a concrete noun, referring to the 'actual thing' that exists materially in the case of printed comics, or digitally in the case of web comics. To this extent the very term itself addresses important shifts in the changing technologies of production.

Key terms

There are a large number of different terms used for the various types of Comics, and though it may appear that they are synonymous, this is not the case. The term 'Comics' is, as I have explained earlier, an umbrella term for the form as a whole (see Figure 1.1). We can use it to describe any of the texts that come under the umbrella of the form itself. Of course, this is not without issues. Marc Singer suggests that the word is 'a relic of the days when the most popular and prominent comics were humorous newspaper strips', adding that 'it may seem particularly ill suited for the earnest memoirs, hard-hitting reportage, and deadly serious superhero narratives that most interest academics today' (2019: 20). The suggestion that Comics has a homonymic relationship to 'comedy' is an uncomfortable one, even though it may be linguistically sensible; indeed, the word has not yet lost the connotations that result from this homonymic relationship. Many scholars have suggested other terms in order to break away from these connections. For example, in their special issue

Figure 1.1 'Umbrella' by Rozi Hathaway (2019).

of *Modern Fiction Studies*, Hillary Chute and Marianne DeKoven chose to use the term 'graphic narrative', although they use it interchangeably with Comics (2006: 767). Some have suggested 'graphica' or 'graphia' to highlight the visual element of the form, while seeking to avoid negative connotations of the term (see Kuskin, 2008 and Weida, 2011). Many artists working in self-published Comics in the 1960s and 1970s favour 'Comix', with the 'x' as a nod to the adult 'x-rated' content of the works themselves. In his afterword to a special issue of *Critical Inquiry*, W.J.T. Mitchell promotes Art Spiegelman's 'co-mix', which, he claims 'is an attractive alternative to comics' (2014: 260). He continues:

> [Co-mix] is a hybrid term for the mixture of media and genre named by comics. And if one looks at the word from the perspective of comics, one can imagine all the co's that

might go into the mix: coordination, cooptation, coincidence, collision, cooperation, comingling of words and images, sound and sight. […] Co-mix foregrounds the comics' tendency to treat words as visual elements, the look of letters as graphic signs, trading in an eye for an ear, as [Marshall] McLuhan put it. It applies to both the generic and mediatic sides of the question and shows the place where genres and media become confused, defying any singular identity confined to their specific history in mass print media, while simultaneously remembering that history, keeping it alive in the homonym, the soundpun of comics/co-mix.

(Mitchell, 2014: 260)

Mitchell's understanding of the nuances of Comics in relation to the 'cos' underscores the complexity of both the form itself and the challenge of naming it. His *penchant* for 'co-mix', however short-lived it may be, is predicated on the word's ability to embrace these contradictions and convolutions, to force us to break with our preexisting understandings of the word and reframe it in light of the contemporary, developing form. The unconventional spelling may be the trigger point for this fracture, but the use of the more familiar term 'Comics' performs a similar reframing, especially when paired with works like Singer's 'serious' texts. It is for this reason that the term retains its popularity within Comics Studies insofar as it creates a space that enables scholars to interrogate the 'thing' itself. Here, I give brief definitions of three other key terms, with signposts to more information in other chapters. There are some definitions that are not given here – *Bandes dessinées*, *Manga*, and *Fumetti*, for example – and these can be found in Chapter 3.

Comic strips

What we now think of as a comic strip was largely born in the pages of large-circulation newspapers (see Chapter 2). In an Anglophone context, the first comic strips appeared in the late nineteenth century, with Richard Outcault's *Hogan's Alley* being credited as the first; Outcault's most famous creation is 'The Yellow Kid', who appeared in February 1895. The same period gave birth to *The Katzenjammer Kids* (1897–2006), created by Rudolph Dirks, and George Herriman's *Krazy Kat* (1913–1944). Despite their amusing content and often colourful presentation, newspaper strips were not initially for younger readers. Jared Gardner writes:

> All of these early strips were addressed first and foremost to adult readers [...] From *Mutt and Jeff* through *Gasoline Alley* the assumption was that daily strips were read by adults and rarely followed regularly by younger readers.
>
> (2015: 246)

Rather than being juvenile, many of these narratives were 'short stories of modern life that could be rewound, slowed down, replayed' (Gardner, 2015: 242). These strips were often experimental and form-defining, as will be discussed further in Chapter 2.

A strip is a short, typically horizontal line of connected images that tell a complete story and, usually, end with a punch line. This punch line can be funny – in the case of long-running strips such as *Marmaduke* (1954–2015) or *Li'l Abner* (1934–1977) – or politically charged, as in *Doonesbury* (1970–present). Though it may seem at the outset that comic strips are the short story analogue of a graphic novel's full-length novel, this is not strictly true. A short story is typically a discrete narrative, and comic strips can be read in a similar fashion as individual stories but they are likely to exist as part of a wider series. The strip can be read in isolation, but will include side references or jokes that make sense only to those who have read the entire series. Regular readers will know that Garfield loves lasagne and hates Mondays (*Garfield*, Davis, 1967–present); they will laugh when General Halftrack makes spelling errors in his instructions (*Beetle Bailey*, Walker et al., 1950–present). These are examples of long-running, widely read strips that have been able to build both their jokes and readership over many years. On occasion, artists write multi-episode short narratives for the purposes of topical or political satire. One such example is Steve Bell, whose strip *If...* has been published in *The Guardian* since 1981. As I am writing this, the strip is following the ongoing COVID-19 pandemic and the Conservative government's action in managing the situation. In late March 2020, news outlets reported that mountain goats were roaming freely around the north Wales town of Llandudno. Bell has framed this 'goat infestation' as a caprine takeover of the government, now called GOAT (Government of All Talents), with wild-eyed beasts pulling the strings in conversation with MPs. The jokes are dependent on the reader's understanding of both the pandemic and the UK government's reaction to it; the series must be read in order, with none missing, in order to make sense. Speaking in broad terms, the jokes in comic strips, be they one-offs or part of a running gag, are often reliant on cultural knowledge and social cues that are specific to the individual strip's target readership.

The construction of a strip relies heavily on its brevity. To have a short space in which to make one's point concentrates the narrative considerably. However, this is not to say that the quality of the artwork needs to be sacrificed. Many long-running strips are skilfully drawn, and artists develop a signature style in the same manner as those of longer works. As an example, let us look briefly at the work of Tom Gauld, whose strips are regularly featured in *The Guardian, The New Yorker,* and *New Scientist.* Many of Gauld's strips are explicitly literary or scientific; they are aimed at adult readers, using wordplay and a bold, simple visual style to deliver his punchline effectively. Figure 1.2 is an excellent example of this coming together of the simple, the witty, and the brief: the uncluttered frames in bold colour, recognisable visual style, and joke that pivots on the often-misused word 'literally' demonstrate the facets of a strip that make it one of the most enduring of the different types of comic.

Graphic novels

The second key term 'graphic novels', is, of all the terms used in Comics, perhaps the most contentious. Typically, a graphic novel is one longer narrative contained within one book or, as the artist

Figure 1.2 'Mindblowing' by Tom Gauld (2018).

Art Spiegelman has it, 'long comic books that require a book-mark' (Spiegelman, 2011). It can be used to describe a bound volume that brings together a previously serialised story; these are usually referred to as trade paperbacks or 'TPBs'. According to most histories, the first graphic novel is Will Eisner's 1978 *A Contract with God*. Indeed, this book's use of the term is often given credit for its adoption in publishing. However, it was used on three separate texts in 1976: Richard Corben's *Bloodstar*, George Metzger's *Beyond Time and Again,* and Jim Steranko's *Chandler: Red Tide*. Since the late-1970s, the term has been used to describe a range of texts of various lengths, and in the twenty-first century, the graphic novel has come into its own as a distinct subgenre of the Comics form.

It is crucial to note that this term is not a synonym for Comics: all graphic novels are comics, but not all comics are graphic novels. Of course, the term itself is tricky. In journalistic terms 'Graphic' can connote a phenomenon that is 'violent or sexually explicit' as much as 'image-driven'; 'novel' refers to a fictional narrative form that has its own complex social and literary history. A large number of graphic novels are neither violent, nor sexually explicit, and not fictional too. Furthermore, the term has been derided by scholars and creators alike for being snobbish and pretentious, used to bestow legitimacy and to create a line of division between comics that are worthy of study and those that are not. Neil Gaiman makes this point when he talks about being told by a reviewer that he wrote graphic novels, not comic books: '[he] felt like someone who'd been informed that she wasn't actually a hooker; that in fact she was a lady of the evening' (Gaiman, in Bender, 1999: 32).

According to Jan Baetens and Hugo Frey's *The Graphic Novel: An Introduction*, graphic novels 'display genuinely significant, although rarely absolute, variation from pre-existing comics and comix traditions' (2015: 3); the term exists as more than just a marketing category. Their definition foregrounds storytelling, making it distinct from political cartooning or single-image caricatures, while also being acutely aware of other aspects such as content and distribution (Baetens and Frey, 2015: 7–8). Unlike mainstream comics, which, as we will see in Chapter 4, follow a 'direct marketing' distribution model, graphic novels tend to be published within the traditional bookseller model. The artist pitches the book to a publishing company, sometimes via an agent, and the publisher offers a deal: typically, the artist creates the work and the publisher controls the publication and distribution process. Comics historian Christina Meyer emphasises that many graphic novels began as serialised stories, sold in magazine format, or as a supplement to another publication, as is the case with Posy Simmonds' 'updated' adaptations of classic novels; this is akin to the serialisation of novels that was popular in the nineteenth century (Meyer, 2015: 273). This different way of promoting and publishing graphic novels is likely to have a large impact on the readership, as well as on matters of print quality, binding, price point, and marketing of the work, all of which affect the themes and stories they contain. While it is clear that the term is not accepted fully, the understanding of 'graphic novel' as more than just a snobbish way of saying an 'expensive comic book,' to paraphrase Alan Moore, is becoming more acceptable (Moore, in Baetens and Frey, 2015: 2). As the entire form continues to evolve and develop, so too will our understanding of the graphic novel, and it is likely that the definition will be further refined to provide a clearer description of various examples and the discourses used to analyse them.

Digital and web comics

The third basic term, which addresses advances within the sphere of information technology, is 'digital and web comics'. With the advent of e-readers and screen-centric engagement with popular culture, Comics is increasingly moving off the printed page and into new media forms. Digital comics and web comics are not exactly the same thing. Digital comics refers to any comic that is disseminated digitally, whether it is via eBook format, a reading app, social media, or online. The primary focus here is on what might be called their method of delivery and the platforms they use. Web comics is a subcategory of this larger division – comics that are published on websites or social media. There are a number of advantages that come with digital comics, including ease of distribution, the ability to make them accessible to disabled readers by means of adding adjustable font sizes or working in tandem with existing accessibility software, for example, and lower production costs. It is important to remember that there is a distinct difference between comics that are created to be disseminated digitally and digitised print comics: Thierry Groensteen argues that the latter involves a shift in the way the reader engages with the comic and that reading digital comics 'entails the loss of a very strong, affectively charged object relation' (2013: 65). Digital comics are not physical and therefore the 'object relation' (the relationship the reader has to the material thing) is by definition going to be different. However, this does not mean that they are not able to create any effect in the reader (see Glossary). It is often thought that digital, especially online, media is evanescent and thus has a reduced affect; when we consider the very real effects of such largely digital phenomena as online trolling and cyberbullying, which has led to victims committing suicide, this is proven not to be the case.

Groensteen is being conservative here in his implicit preference of print versions over digital. While this is a key issue in the understanding of the material object, Kirchoff and Cook suggest that Comics is 'large enough for both print and digital' (2019: 3). Many originally digital comics are making the jump into print form; in many cases the two different forms (print and online) co-exist and serve different audiences to great effect. While technology for digital comics is relatively new and rapidly advancing, there is still a considerably strong market for print forms. They are designed to address audiences who engage with their reading material in a different way; the two are not in competition with each other as much as complementary. Many comics move between print and digital. *American Born Chinese* by Gene Luen Yang began life as a web comic before it was published as a graphic novel in 2006; it became the first comic to be nominated for a National Book Award. In addition, many Comics awards now include categories for digital comics, including the Ignatz Award's 'Outstanding Online Comic' and the Eisner Award's 'Best Digital Comic'.

While print comics exist as material objects that are tangible and physical, digital comics do not – their publication space is therefore distinct from their print cousins in that it is not constrained by paper size, printing technologies, or price. In his 2000 book *Reinventing Comics*, Scott McCloud proposes that the computer monitor, or other digital screen, is not a page, but a window onto an 'infinite canvas' (2000: 222–224). Rather than constraining the comic to pages of a certain size and encouraging a linear movement through them, the artist could give the reader the option to zoom in and out of an infinitely large canvas, changing the way that the reader moves through the narrative. The way that this type of Comics engages with the technology available is demonstrative of the innovation and ground-breaking nature that is now a familiar feature of this form more generally.

Possibly the most important aspect of digital comics, and of web comics specifically, is that the internet provides an opportunity for any individual to create and publish their work without the mediation of an institution such as the publishing industry. Moreover, they can reinvent and develop their style, using the flexibility of the platform to experience, change, adapt, and, potentially, mature. Figure 1.3 shows a comparison of two figures from Jeph Jacques' long-running web comic *Questionable Content*

Figure 1.3 'Faye Cuts to the Chase #4' (2003) and 'Sanitary Condition #3982' (2019) from *Questionable Content* by Jeph Jacques.

from 2003 and 2019 respectively. The difference in style comes not only from Jacques' development as an artist, but also from changes in technology that allow for the comic to be created differently. To a large extent, the digital arena functions to level the playing field because anyone with an internet connection can reach the widest possible audience. There are digital comics on all themes, and in many cases, they become an outlet for minority groups that do not normally enjoy widespread media representation. A 2015 article in the *Hindustan Times* claimed that the huge surge in popularity in Indian web comics was due to the fact that 'most [...] are anti-statusquoist and are keen to speak against unjust social norms' (Verma, 2015: n.p.). The article includes a quotation from an 'avid reader', who suggests that 'web comics have the kind of humour that makes its point without offending people. It doesn't keep the public at arms-length' (Verma, 2015: n.p.). This has proven to be the case internationally, and web comics use the ease of distribution that the internet allows to mobilise the form for all manner of objectives, from diversionary entertainment, to political activism, to product advertising. Given the huge advances that are being made in digital comics technologies, it may be true to say that the bound book is no longer the dominant form. It is the electronic version of an even earlier form, the scroll, that has taken back control after a hiatus of a few thousand years.

Cartoons

If comic strips require a certain level of social and cultural understanding in order to draw out meaning and encourage readers to 'get' the joke, then cartoons probably require even more. A cartoon, in this sense, is a satirical or humorous image or, occasionally, a series of images. The word was originally used for the preparatory drawings for a tapestry, stained glass, or *fresco* (these are also called *modello*). It was first used in a more recognisably modern sense in 1843 in the periodical publication *Punch*, when applied to satirical drawings, especially those by John Leech (Adler and Hill, 2008). Cartoons, specifically political and editorial cartoons, draw on the traditions of visual political commentary that began with the circulation of the engravings of William Hogarth and the sketches of George Townshend. The form developed into a powerful and popular tool in the hands of James Gillray in the late eighteenth century. Historian Chris Upton reminds us that no particular libel laws were in place at this time and so 'the prints of Gillray were scatological, brutal, offensive and witty all in one and no-one, from the King downward, was spared' (2006: n.p.); he wryly adds that 'It was ironic (and only fair) that both the caricaturist and his chief quarry went mad'. The contemporary political cartoon remains a compelling mode to make a statement; the 2005 publication of twelve cartoons depicting Muhammad by *Jyllands-Posten*, a Danish newspaper, and their re-publication in the French comic magazine *Charlie Hebdo* with catastrophic consequences for the French cartoonists, is testament to the power of images as tools for controversy and political comment; I discuss this in more detail in Chapter 6. Cartoons condense their meaning into a single image and caption. The artist uses multiple layers of meaning and social codes to create the images, which are often provocative, being created quickly, and in such a way to allow easy dissemination via printed media such as newspapers, or the internet.

The mechanical and the technical

The panel and the gutter

The basic unit of the comic is the panel – an image within specific spatial parameters that conveys one unit of visual thought or a single concept or idea. Duncan and Smith remind us that this name stands, 'irrespective of whether or not there are actual panel borders' (2009: 131). In order to produce each panel, the creator combines the visual and the verbal to represent the specific moment, thought, or idea in a recognisable way that speaks to other panels. This corresponds with Spiegelman's claim that Comics is closer to poetry than prose because it requires specific, careful, and complex planning. He calls Comics 'very condensed thought structures' (Spiegelman in Campbell, 2008: 61). The most common word that we encounter in Comics Studies when talking about panels is the term 'fragment': a panel is a single visual part of a much larger thing. It cannot exist on its own and still hold its true purpose. However, while the term 'fragment' identifies the single panel, its meaning cannot be isolated; the true purpose of the panel is to connect with others in a sequence that contributes to the overall meaning that the strip generates.

The panel by itself is not a comic; it is merely a building block, just as a single paragraph or chapter is one element in the larger narrative structure of a novel. A related term in the lexicon of Comic Studies is 'gutter' – the space between the images. It is the visual interval between panels that, while seemingly empty, is of central importance to the creation of the essential narrative elements of the form. Thierry Groensteen writes that 'the true magic of comics operates between the images, the tension that binds them' (2007: 41). What goes on in the gutter – Scott McCloud calls it 'closure' – is what drives the narrative forward: 'comics panels fracture both time and space […] but closure allows us to connect these moments and mentally construct a continuous, unified reality' (1994: 74). Barbara Postema considers panels and gutters as constituent parts that 'combine on the comics page to create a synergy that goes beyond the content of the single panel and makes something new'; she reminds us that 'panels need to be considered not just by themselves but in relation to the other panels' (2013: 28). The panel is important because of the relationships that exist within.

We can explain the function of the 'gutter' in the following way: Comics as a form relies on images in sequence for the production of meaning. Therefore, there is something that exists outside that sequence that may be designated as the space that links the images and brings them together as contributors to the overall meaning of the sequence. That 'something' is the gutter. The comic works only because the reader is the agent who makes connections between panels that creates the story. For Paul Gravett, this is a 'leap of faith […] driv[ing] the reader onward'; he adds that closure is 'a hot-wired impulse in humans to forge some sort of meaning between one image and the next' (2013: 30).

The gutter may, as McCloud posits, be tapping into some innate human impulse to build connections but it is also a space of co-creation; it is the locus where creator and reader come together. It is, therefore, much more than blank space. Creators can mobilise the gutter as a space that exists outside of the main narrative where alternative readings and clues about the story can lurk. For example, in her 2012 psychological horror comic *Adamtine*, Hannah Berry uses black gutters to heighten the unease and claustrophobia of her characters' experiences. In an interview she described her use of gutters:

> One of the rules I set myself is that anything that happens within the panels is corporeal; anything that happens outside the panels is somehow supernatural in nature, because what happens is that after a while the blackened gutters and borders start to bleed in, start to interfere in ways with the panels themselves.
>
> (Fitch, 2017: 231)

The gutters begin to affect the story and it is up to the reader to decide how much they wish to integrate them into their reading experience. Figure 1.4 shows a typical layout of a page, with labels to show the different components.

Figure 1.4 This is what a comics page (sometimes) looks like. By Samuel Williams (2019).

The page

The normal experience of reading involves turning pages, where the page is a unit of text. But in Comics Studies the page is problematic to the point where we might ask the question: What is a page? What does it mean to talk about the page and how does this work in Comics? When we think about pages, we are confronted with two distinct categories. On the one hand, the physical object of a book and the pieces of paper it consists of. On the other hand, a webpage or other digital space that is viewable on an electronic device. Let us, for the moment, focus here on the book as a physical object. As with forms such as ergodic literature (see Glossary), where the layout of the page is of specific importance to the overall work, the Comics page is not simply the space in which the story plays out but is also a constitutive medium through which the narrative is created and advanced. Let us look at some examples of how the page can work, and at the terms used to describe elements of this process.

The full-page layout

'Full-page layout' is a clumsy, if descriptive, term for the entirety of what we can see across a single- or double-page spread. Thierry Groensteen uses the word 'hyperframe' to identify the full contents of a page, which includes its outer boundary; he observes that, 'the notion of the hyperframe applies itself to a single unit, which is the page' (2007: 30). The Comics creator is aware of the appearance of the full spread and how the shape of panels can contribute to the furthering of the narrative. Typically, the story will move across the page left-to-right, and down the page in a Z-shaped motion, the action of earlier panels influences later ones. Sometimes the page becomes a ludic space for the characters and, as a consequence, the storyline breaks out of the panels, and the whole story is played out across the whole of the page. This means that, rather than reading left-to-right and top-to-bottom (in a Z shape), the reader will be forced to read all over the page, usually following visual guides and arrows to show the path to follow. A particularly amusing example of this is found in Pascal Jousselin's *Imbattable* series (translated as 'Invincible'), shown in Figure 1.5. The hero is a dumpy little character who uses the form of the comic to save the day, usually by jumping between panels and tiers in order to get ahead of criminals. He is aware of the Comics form and can 'break' the traditional reading structure. Jousselin gives us a visual path to follow – we can see the movement of *Imbattable* himself from his kitchen in the top tier to jumping onto the criminal via the movement lines that connect the panels; similarly, we can follow the passage of the bullets via the movement lines in the final tier to see how the criminal is apprehended. The reader must move in atypical ways, but this is guided by the artist. Not only is *Imbattable* very much aware of the Comics form; his power is intimately bound up with it. His logo is a Comics grid on his jumper; just as Superman

Figure 1.5 Imbattable Tome 1: Justice et Légumes Frais (p. 3) by Pascal Jousselin (2017).

has his iconic 'S', *Imbattable* outwardly displays his 'super power status'. He knows how to manipulate the form itself so that he always wins. In following the path he takes to 'save the day', the reader can see different ways to read the comic itself, as well as how the reading 'path' can change the story.

Page turns

The next issue to consider is 'page turns'. Let us take the example of a crime comic. The bottom right-hand panel of the page shows that the crime is about to be committed: perhaps a victim is cowering in a corner, in sight of their attacker. After turning the page, the top left-hand panel shows a post-fight scene indicating that the attack is over. The action occurs at exactly the same moment as the reader turns the page and so they are complicit in the action because they turned the page. This use of the materiality of the comic and the fact that the reader pushes the story along as they turn pages is highly effective, not only in crime comics but also in all kinds of stories. It brings the reader into the action by making us an active participant, if not fully complicit. The page turn becomes a constitutive element of the story, not just a mechanical necessity but a storytelling device in its own right.

Bleeds and splash pages

An eagle-eyed reader may have noticed that both Comics Studies and the Comics industry tends to borrow terms from other industries in order to explain physical and thematic aspects of the form. This is nowhere truer than in the two terms. Both are used in Graphic Design and printing to discuss the physical object and the placement of images. In basic terms, a bleed is an image that is printed to the very edge of the page, with no border; this is sometimes referred to as a 'full bleed'. Bleeds can play various roles within stories, especially as narrative devices that relate to the representation of time. Scott McCloud writes, 'time is no longer contained by the familiar lines of the closed panel, but instead haemorrhages and escapes into timeless space' (1994: 130). I have argued elsewhere that

Bleeds are, by their nature, violent. The image's domination of the page is striking and demands the reader's complete attention. The absence of frames on the page edges removes any sense of constriction or confinement – the image has total control of the page.

(2017: 49)

An example of the mobilisation of the violence of bleeds is Frank Miller's comic *300* (1998), which depicts the Second Persian invasion of Greece; the whole story is depicted in bleeds that span double pages.

Also, while a splash page is usually a bleed, not all bleeds are splash pages. Splash pages usually appear at the beginning of a story and are largely decorative, used to establish a sense of location or temporal setting. They may also be used to show off the artistic skill of the creators. Duncan and Smith point out that 'a splash page seldom depicts the climax of a story' and that they are more often 'a pin-up of the hero leaping into action' (2009: 139).

The balloon and the bubble

Comics is primarily an image-driven form, but this is not to say that words do not feature or, indeed, matter. Having said that, the ways in which words are presented, as well as *what* is presented, are important. One of the most recognisable aspects of the comic that has almost become a visual synecdoche for Comics as a whole is the balloon (also known as the 'bubble'). The bubble is typically presented as a rounded, white space on the page, in which speech or thought is written (see Figure 1.4). Catherine Khordoc observes that 'the balloon is at once what separates and what brings together text and image', calling it an 'effective method of creating "sound" effects in a textual medium' (2001: 157). The balloon, whether it contains speech or thought, gives the reader information in two ways: by its physical presence and by the words that the balloon contains. By its presence we already know that the characters are communicating to us something we need to know; the directional pointer of the balloon shows us which character to look to specifically. Furthermore, the outline can give a hint to its content. A smooth-lined balloon is typical for ordered speech at a normal volume; a jagged balloon can denote screaming or that the sound is coming from an electronic source; a broken line can denote whispers; a balloon with curled edges followed by a series of descending small circles indicates the 'silent speech' or the thought of the character to whom the balloon is pointing. In these ways the reader is given a solid understanding of the contents of the bubble before they read the words it contains. Typically, we expect the contents to be words but this is not always the case. If a character is swearing, the balloon may include grawlixes (typographical symbols used to replace swearing, such as '!!?#@&!?$!'). An ellipsis may denote a pointed silence or a moment of confusion. Most unusually, artists like Jason use pictures within their balloons; a character asking for a cup of coffee may utter an image of a coffee cup, as in Jason's *Sshhhh!* (2002). Even if we do find that bubbles contain words, an artist may choose to use different fonts or diacritics, typographical markings such as accents that denote a change in the pronunciation of a letter, to represent different tones, accents, or even languages. In the *Astérix* series by Uderzo and Goscinny, characters are represented with different fonts and diacritics to show that they are speaking different languages, a technique that is used to great comic effect: in one example, a particular joke involves a Viking dog, which barks in Nordic ('wøøf'!).

Though we may think of the balloon as being ubiquitous within the form, historically speaking this has not always been the case. In early examples, words were confined to labels positioned beneath the panels. For Thierry Smolderen, '[the label] evoked the self-presentational written banners of the frozen *tableau vivant*. It was in its nature to be embedded in static coded pictures cut [off] from the physical world' (qtd in Gravett, 2013: 26). Such was the resistance to the integration of bubbles, especially in Europe, that American imports such as *The Katzenjammer Kids*, *Felix the Cat*, and *Mickey Mouse* would have 'their speech balloons [removed] and replaced by commentary below, sometimes in rhyme' (Gravett, 2013: 26). However, this is no longer the case, and the balloon is internationally used, recognised, and understood.

In his guide to writing and drawing comics, Will Eisner calls the balloon a 'desperation device [which] attempts to capture and make visible an ethereal element: sound' (2008a: 24). This statement may make more sense to those familiar with Eisner's work since in many of his comics, speech is an integral part of the image, artistically woven into the fabric of the panel and not placed within a balloon. Regardless of Eisner's view, the balloon performs a vital function within the comics' narrative, clearly defining and representing the various levels of the panel and the image in a way that is instantly recognisable. A balloon is the Comics version of the mousetrap: build a new one if you can but the old one continues to be the most effective way of capturing speech.

2   Histories

The earliest forms of storytelling deployed visual images rather than words. Before 'writing', there were pictograms and diagrams that told bold stories in order to communicate cultural and social truths. Arguably the oldest example of drawing can be found in the Blombos Cave, located in South Africa, which dates from around 73,000 BCE, though we cannot say for certain whether these drawings were narrative in intention or purely decorative. What we can be certain of is that they were representational (Nelson, 2015: 8). Even so, there *are* clear examples of the use of pictures to tell stories that pre-date other narrative forms, including cave art found on all continents, tomb paintings, and petroglyphs. The foundations of writing systems developed alongside a rich pictorial history which can be traced back over thousands of years to simple pictograms. These can be found in every culture across the globe and they have developed into the myriad systems we now use (Robinson, 1995). Without exaggeration we can say that, as soon as humans could make marks on surfaces, stories were being told and visually represented.

Human beings formulate their experiences through stories, producing narratives that enable them to explain and understand the social and historical contexts in which they live. It is a central part of how we understand and develop both our own identities and our relationships with others. According to Jerome Bruner, 'that which we call the world is a product of some mind whose symbolic procedures construct [it]' (1985: 95). The 'symbolic procedures' that form the basis of this construction are socially

Figure 2.1 Close-up of the marble relief on Trajan's Column by Allison
Kidd and the Institute for the Study of the Ancient World.
License: CC BY 2.0 (2011).

and culturally determined but the act of storytelling itself remains
constant. Similarly, telling stories with images is universal and
can be recognised across cultures. Trajan's Column in Rome is
a good example (see Figure 2.1). Completed in 113 CE, at first
glance the 30-metre tall marble column, topped with a statue
of St Peter, may not appear to be in any way related to Comics.
However, the column features a 190-metre spiralling frieze that
tells the story of the Roman-Dacian Wars (101–102 CE and
105–106 CE). It is an impressive monument that tells the story
of military prowess, and, as a symbol of the strength of Rome,
it is powerful. It demands no deep understanding of Latin and
the story it tells cuts across the many territories of the Roman
Empire and its trading partners (Darville, 2008: 224). To take

another example, we can look at the Bayeux Tapestry, a 70-metre long embroidered cloth that depicts the events of the Norman Conquest, culminating in the 1066 Battle of Hastings and the death of King Harold I. George Wingfield Digby writes that, 'It was designed to tell a story to a largely non-literate public; it is like a strip cartoon, racy, emphatic, colourful, with a good deal of blood and thunder and some ribaldry' (1957: 37). It is most certainly racy – there are, according to Prof George Garnett of the University of Oxford, 93 visible penises (2018: n.p.). As with Trajan's Column, the tapestry is a statement of military success and political machination, as well as a public statement designed to glorify and celebrate the victor. The narrative pictorialises particular episodes in a 'history' of significant events, choosing what we remember, while excluding other parts of the story. Monuments of this kind fulfil a memorial function in that they reflect the achievements, military and otherwise, of particular cultures. We might connect this process of representation with something like Percy Bysshe Shelley's poem 'Ozymandias' that celebrates a 'fragment' of a monument and uses the remains to moralise on the futility of power. The poem takes the remains of a monument and makes a story out of it.

A third example plays on the fondness for gore and titillation that one may associate with tabloid newspapers but can be traced throughout the history of narrative works from Ancient Greek theatre, through Chaucer, to Shakespeare, and beyond. Religious murals depicting the afterlife can be seen in places of worship, especially churches, and many of them depict terrifying visions of hell. One particularly grisly example is Giovanni di Pietro Falloppi's doom painting on the wall of the Basilica di San Petronio in Bologna. A blue Satan dominates the image, his two mouths chewing on sinners, while others around him are tortured and maimed by demons. This representation of hell evokes Dante and the torments of the sinners in the frozen river Cocytus (see Dante, *Inferno*, cantos 32–34). To a largely non-literate church-going populace, who were accustomed to the image of hellfire and eternal damnation as deterrents from earthly sin, paintings such as this one would be powerful and dissuasive visualisations of things to come. Though this example differs in both theme and intention from my earlier two, it is still partisan storytelling represented in the form of visual images. Of course, the problem with these three examples is their distinct lack of physical portability (cf. Sabin 1996). These are single items to which the viewer must travel, and they are designed to make statements in particular static locations. This is not to suggest that their stasis makes these artefacts less important, but that their use as tools of communication is limited to specific geographic locations.

The early history of written storytelling and of Comics' visual predecessors are, in many respects, similar, and their concerns overlap: the storyteller finds a way to inscribe the story on a cave wall, stone, papyrus, vellum, or paper in ways that are understandable initially through image and drawing. But, as writing systems developed, cultures gradually broke away from simple pictorial representation. As a result, although visual images did not become obsolete, their relationship to storytelling gradually began to change with written verbal narratives becoming dominant. The now-ubiquitous novel is generally accepted to have begun in English with Daniel Defoe's *Robinson Crusoe* in 1719 (see Watt, 2001). However, there are a number of Elizabethan 'novels' (including Nashe's *Pierce Penniless, His Supplication to the Divell*, published in 1592) and a long tradition of 'chronicle history' that goes back to Latin models, beginning with books such as Bede's *Ecclesiastical History of the English People* (c. 731). The point here is that narratives sometimes do not take explicitly the fictional form, though they may contain elements of what we would call fiction. Print technologies were changing the way that texts worked and were disseminated. At the same time, adult literacy rates grew rapidly throughout the eighteenth and nineteenth centuries, in the wake of the growth of interest in education reforms for the working classes, though formal education was sporadic, and remained so in Britain until the 1944 Education Act.

Developments in printing, literacy, and the availability of material made this shift in literacy possible. And as these developments happened, visual culture in all of its manifestations proceeded alongside a developing print culture. Though image narratives do require the viewer to have a specific level of literacy, it is not the same as written literacy and can be taught and transmitted without 'formal' education; image narratives are therefore able to transcend educational and language barriers within a society or cultural group. Often, their inclusion was aimed at providing information and narrative decoration for the masses. Visual images decorate the walls and windows of churches and temples; they also represent elements of a Christian narrative played out on the walls of tombs and palaces; indeed, our art galleries are full of examples of large tableaux that tell particular stories. This does not, of course, mean that they are Comics; indeed, there are many aspects of the Comics form that are missing from this kind of art. The following section will introduce three examples of what I have called 'proto-comics'. These are not strictly comics in the modern sense of the term but they reveal techniques and aspects that are clearly recognisable and which have developed into the form we know today. The focus in this chapter is on Anglophone works but Chapter 3 will discuss international histories.

Proto-comics

Eighteenth-century Europe was a world in flux. Populations were becoming more diverse due to immigration and more informed due to early attempts at educational reform, while tensions between countries developed into geopolitical struggles. Toward the end of the century, the French Revolution and its immediate aftermath affected all of Europe, bringing to the fore deep-rooted and widespread social turmoil. This was a fertile environment for political comment; the public's taste for politically charged prose essays, printed in pamphlets or newspapers, extended well into the realm of visual representation. Political cartooning blossomed as a popular medium, with images often appearing alongside prose narratives, and there was also a rise in the use of humorous art to lampoon public figures (especially politicians), to make comment, and to pass judgment on topical issues.

Probably the most important figure who produced these early graphic narratives was William Hogarth (1697–1764). Born to a middle-class London family, he became an apprentice engraver at a young age. He was fond of sketching the people he saw in the streets of London and developed a keen eye for creating bustling, metropolitan scenes with a sharp satirical edge. It has been suggested that his father's imprisonment for unpaid debts, following a rather unusual business venture in which he opened a Latin-speaking coffee house, informed the young Hogarth's views (Paulson, 1991: 26). Later in life, he became a successful engraver and artist in his own right and developed a significant following. The writer and social commentator Charles Lamb wrote of Hogarth's images that they were, in fact, books that '[teemed with] fruitful, suggestive meaning of words. Other pictures we look at; his pictures we read' (1811: 82). For Hogarth, art was an effective way of transmitting moral education. He did not aim for pictorial realism, but opted instead to use carica-ture that involved the grotesque exaggeration of features. This allowed him to use bawdy, often obscene, imagery to attract the attention of his viewers while also making bold statements about human behaviour and its social and cultural repercussions.

There were five sequences of 'moral works', to use their general collective name, the first of which Hogarth completed in 1731. 'A Harlot's Progress' is a six-scene series of paintings (published as engravings in 1732) that tells the story of the ill-fated Moll Hackabout. When we first meet Moll, she is portrayed talking with a brothel madam, who is seeking to lure her into sex work. Throughout the central scenes, Moll goes from being a kept woman and wife of a wealthy merchant to a poverty-stricken sex worker, imprisoned in Bridewell Prison, before she finally contracts Syphilis and dies. The narrative is unashamedly grim in its revelation of the established moral corruption that contributes to Moll's ultimate downfall. Thierry Smolderen describes the engravings as highly charged documents that reveal large amounts of information about the mores, customs, ethics, and politics of eighteenth-century England (2014: 3–23). The series was a roaring success and, in 1735, a 'sequel', 'A Rake's Progress', appeared. In the eight scenes of this work we see the life of Tom Rakewell, who squanders his inheritance on luxury, gambling, and orgies, before dying alone and insane in the infamous Royal Bethlem Hospital (more famously known as Bedlam). Neither sequence is subtle in the clear moral message it seeks to communicate: degenerate living will lead to a tragic end.

As Inge suggests, these images are not to be casually glanced at but 'require full attention […] there are no narrative guides and no spoken words, so the story is implied entirely in the visuals' (2017: 10). They establish a clear story told in pictures but lack the combination of word and image that we would now consider necessary to classify them as Comics. Nevertheless, as Inge argues, 'what is indisputable […] is the powerful influence Hogarth had on all efforts to tell stories through pictures in all visual narrative to come, including comics' (2017: 11). Hogarth's contemporaries and artistic successors exerted far-reaching influence across Europe and North America. Later in this book, I will discuss the first North American cartoon, attributed to Benjamin Franklin, but before that we need to examine the contributions of a number of other artists whose impact is also important; they include James Gillray (1756–1815), Thomas Rowlandson (1756–1827), and Thomas Nast (1840–1902), to name but three. The most important and influential of the day's cartoons would be disseminated internationally as well as reproduced in political pamphlets.

Of course, Hogarth's work had a didactic function as well as a political one, since much of it aimed to teach moral lessons despite the fact that it was directed at a predominantly adult readership. Nevertheless, his works are funny and eye-catching, with much about them that entertains. They lay the groundwork for those who began to develop the 'modern comic' but if we were to appoint a 'father of the comic strip', the obvious forerunner would be Rodolphe Töpffer (1799–1846), a Swiss schoolteacher whose self-published short comic strips were the products of his own imagination, though he seems to have had models among older progenitors of the Comics form. Töpffer did not create his strips for publication but to entertain his friends and students, and he found an unlikely champion in the person of the German writer Johann Wolfgang von Goethe. Although Goethe was well-known for his dislike of satirical caricature, he was effusive in his praise for Töpffer's *Adventures of Doctor Festus*:

[Töpffer] really sparkles with talent and wit; much of it is quite perfect; it shows just how much the artist could yet achieve, if he dealt with modern [or less frivolous] material and went to work with less haste, and more reflection. If Töpffer did not have such an insignificant text [i.e., story-line] before him, he would invent things which could surpass all our expectations.

(Qtd in Soret, 1929: 489)

It was with the encouragement and enthusiastic patronage of his unusual admirer that, in 1833, Töpffer began to publish. In time, seven stories were published in newspapers across Europe and North America. The first, written in 1831, is *Histoire de M. Jabot*, the story of a dandy who tries to enter upper-class society (see Figure 2.2). David Kunzle writes that 'Jabot the social upstart was a safe, broadly recognisable satirical target, a familiar stereotype of Restoration satire' and goes on to call the figure a 'little buffoon rising from below' (2007: 59). In *M. Jabot*, as in all Töpffer's works, we can see the beginnings of panels and captions, although it contains no speech and thought bubbles, that might confirm its status as a comic and mark a shift in the development of the form from Hogarth's wordless scenes.

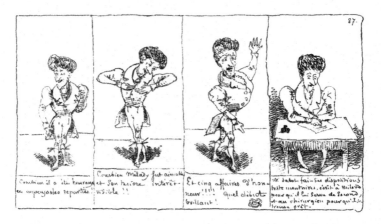

Figure 2.2 'Histoire de Monsieur Jabot' by Rodolphe Töpffer (1833).

Töpffer's influence stretched far beyond his native Switzerland with the 1842 publication of *Histoire de M. Vieux Bois* in the US, under the title of *The Adventures of Mr. Obadiah Oldbuck*. The publication came in the form of a supplement to the New York newspaper *Brother Jonathan* and, according to Robert Beerbohm, is the first comic book published in the US (Gabillet, 2010: 32). Inge points out that 'this holds true, of course, only if we consider *Obadiah Oldbuck* indeed a comic book' (2017: 11). This was a popular book, and Paul Gravett recounts the story of a copy being found among the belongings of Lewis Carroll after his death that provides confirmation for the reference in *Alice in Wonderland* to Alice's love for comics in the form that we recognise:

> In the opening paragraph [of *Alice's Adventures in Wonderland*] a listless Alice famously grumbled, 'where is the use of a book without pictures or conversations?' She would probably have loved reading comics, curiosities filled with imagery and often abuzz with noisy speech balloons.
>
> (2007: 621)

This reference to *Obadiah Oldbuck*, embedded in a work of popular children's literature, is a testament to the far-reaching impact of Töpffer's work.

There is one final early comic worthy of mention in relation to the issue of 'firsts': *The Glasgow Looking-Glass* (11 June 1825 – 3 April 1826). *The Glasgow Looking-Glass* was probably the first mass-produced magazine to tell stories using images and, as such, may be regarded as the earliest comic. It was the brainchild of English artist William Heath, who had fled to Glasgow to avoid his creditors, and lithographer John Watson; Laurence Grove makes the amusing point that the idea was probably conceived in 'one of the city's drinking dens' (2016: n.p.). After five issues, the title was changed to *The Northern Looking-Glass*, to 'reflect a more national coverage of events in Scotland' (University of Glasgow Library, 2005: n.p.). The focus of these issues remained on life in Glasgow, albeit in a satirised and distorted way. Heath not only commented on politics and leading news events, but also poked fun at fashion, leisure pursuits, and people at all strata of society. A common vehicle for humour (and horror!) was medical education, with a large number of comics and cartoons featuring medical students doing morally dubious and agonising things to their patients. This is unsurprising, given that many of Heath's readers were educated people and Scotland was home to several medical schools of renown.

The magazine ran for only nineteen issues, a tenure that was not uncommon for such publications at the time; indeed, very few of these publications lasted for longer than three years, with the notable exception being the periodical magazine *Punch*, which ran from 1841 until its eventual closure in 2002. But, despite the brevity of its ten-month existence, *The Glasgow Looking-Glass* made some ground-breaking and form-defining additions to the contemporaneous comic. The first known strip, 'History of a Coat', ran for several instalments as the coat was passed from owner to owner in each issue. Unlike other contenders for the title of 'first', *The Glasgow Looking-Glass* contains some recognisably 'Comics' features: speech bubbles are used in conversations in a way that modern readers will immediately recognise, and some stories end with 'To be continued', imitating the serialised publication of novels. It stands as one of the earliest — if not *the* earliest — works of its type and a landmark text in the history of Comics.

We can see how Comics are beginning to take the shape that we recognise through the works we have discussed so far. The salient elements are: stories told in panels, serialisation, the use of captions, and the emergence of a clear narrative flow. The following section takes us closer to the form with which we are familiar and discusses newspaper comics and the eventual rise of the 'mainstream'.

The newsstand boom and the mainstream

Comics became a regular fixture in newspapers in the late nineteenth century. Inspired by Töpffer, emerging artists in Europe and North America began to experiment and develop their own versions of Töpffer's strips. In 1865, German author and caricaturist Wilhelm Busch created *Max und Moritz*, about two troublesome boys. The book consisted of seven moral tales, similar to German children's stories such as Heinrich Hoffmann's *Struwwelpeter* (1845). The final part of the book shows the boys being thrown into a sack of grain, ground down in the mill, and eaten by geese. The gruesome and extreme nature of the stories was designed to make the moral points bolder and more memorable, although this may be debated by some. Busch's stories were an obvious influence for the types of comics that were to come, and especially those which began to appear in newspapers in the 1890s. It is important to note that, while the works of writers such as Busch and Hoffmann may have been aimed at younger readers, the majority of newspaper strips that drew inspiration from them were not (see Lefèvre, 2017: 22; Gardner, 2012: 2). Though their protagonists were young people, the themes and execution were not always appropriate for children.

For those living in the nascent US of the 1890s, it is likely that newspaper choice was in some way influenced by the comics that it printed. Printing technologies were developing quickly to allow for more complex prints to be made faster and more cheaply; colour printing had not previously been as widespread and was certainly not to be wasted but its use became more and more prevalent until a full-colour, full-page Sunday comic was the norm. Moreover, these comics were big: they received a full page on Sundays, and daily strips tended to fill the width of the page. The artwork was often detailed and aesthetically pleasing, created entirely by hand. One of the most popular newspaper offerings of the day was Richard F. Outcault's *Hogan's Alley*, a series set in a New York City slum, populated by eccentric characters and urchins. The central character of the strip was Mickey Dugan, better known as 'The Yellow Kid'. Mickey was depicted as a bald, barefoot, buck-toothed little boy in a hand-me-down yellow nightshirt; his words often appeared on the nightshirt instead of in bubbles. Outcault provided the following context for Mickey:

> The Yellow Kid was not an individual but a type. When I used to go about the slums on newspaper assignments,

I would encounter him often, wandering out of doorways or sitting down on dirty doorsteps. I always loved the Kid. He had a sweet character and a sunny disposition and was generous to a fault. Malice, envy or selfishness were not traits of his, and he never lost his temper.

(Outcault, qtd in Blackbeard, 1995: 135)

Mickey's popularity extended beyond his slum existence and he became a heart-warming, cute character. Indeed, Sabine Doran notes the importance of the *Yellow Kid* (as the strip was renamed) in the newspaper battles of *fin de siècle* New York City:

In the battle between [Joseph] Pulitzer and the upstart [William] Hearst, the migration of *The Yellow Kid* to Hearst's daily *New York Press* in 1897 (seen as a real coup at the time) gave rise to the term 'yellow kid journalism' which evolved into 'yellow journalism' [a name for sensationalist and often poorly-researched reporting, as found in Hearst's publication].

(2013: 11)

Comic strips moved between publications as artists were headhunted, often with much more generous terms of employment; if publishers knew that a certain strip was likely to bring in many new readers, they would pay handsomely to secure the rights to it. It is difficult to suggest a modern comparison to this migration but a close comparison, in terms of magnitude and revenue, might be Disney's acquisition of the Star Wars franchise in 2012 (BBC, 2012: n.p.). The comparison demonstrates the importance of comic strips to newspaper readership at the time. The *Yellow Kid* was not the only popular story of this period. *The Katzenjammer Kids*, created by Rudolph Dirks in 1897, ran in the Sunday supplement of Hearst's *New York Journal* and remained in print until 2006, making it the longest-running comic strip of all time (109 years). Dirks' strip was, like Outcault's, involved in the Hearst-Pulitzer rivalry. When Dirks wanted to leave the *Journal* in 1912, he was officially denied a release from his contract but left anyway, leading to a long and convoluted legal battle involving the strip's new artist, Harold Knerr. Dirks went on to create an almost identical strip, *The Captain and the Kids*, for Pulitzer. Comic strips were developing as an integral part of newspapers at the same time that newspapers were emerging as commercial and competitive enterprises. Strips were often important in driving sales and increasing readership, which in turn played into advertising revenue and the financial continuation of the publication. As such, these strips were directly aimed at adults who comprised the newspapers' main readership. Comics as primarily a children's form (in an American context) developed later, as I discuss in due course.

All newspapers saw the financial advantage that came with a popular strip. In 1913, the *New York Evening Journal*, another Hearst publication, launched *Krazy Kat*. This strip used surreal, often bizarre, humour and featured Krazy, a simple-minded cat who was madly in love with Ignatz, a mouse. Ignatz repays Krazy's adoration by flinging bricks at their head (I say 'their' because Krazy is never definitively male or female). The love triangle is complete with the arrival of Officer Pupp, who is in love with Krazy (Figure 2.3). The art of *Krazy Kat* may be simple and the humour largely slapstick but the strip developed a dedicated following. Despite being drawn for a more general audience, as evinced by the slapstick humour, the off-beat stories and quirky presentation led to a large number of 'intellectual' fans, including the poet e.e. cummings and the art theorist Gilbert Seldes. Though this strip was popular, it did not have the same popularity as others that appeared at the same time. However, it is regularly cited as an influence by modern cartoonists and both the visual and verbal wit and creativity have served to establish it as a germinal artistic production from this period.

In the UK at this time, comics served a different purpose and readership. Chris Murray writes that 'with a rapidly increasing market for mass publication in the late nineteenth century, the scene was set for a dramatic expansion of genre publishing' (2017: 45). Satirical magazines remained popular and Ally Sloper, one of the earliest recurring characters in comics, appeared in *Judy* in 1867. Sloper was the creation of Charles Henry Ross and his wife, the pseudonymous Marie Duval, and it has been

Figure 2.3 Excerpt from 'Krazy Kat' by George Herriman (1922).

suggested that he was among the inspirations for Charlie Chaplin's 'little tramp' (Sabin, 1993). The character was lazy and work-shy, with a large fan following in both the working class and the middle class with the result that a stand-alone publication was launched in 1884, *Ally Sloper's Half-Holiday*. Although Ally Sloper was a very popular character, the publication did not sell as well as expected. However, what did sell in huge numbers was the 'penny dreadful'. Cheaply printed on low-quality paper, and featuring lurid stories of horror and crime, the penny dreadful has been hailed as being among the first examples of a popular form aimed directly at young people (Springhall, 1999). As one might expect, these publications faced many of the same criticisms as all media aimed at young people, and they were the root of many outbursts of moral panic, suggesting that the violent stories they contained would result in murder and depravity (Anglo, 1977).

Their popularity was challenged in 1890, with the launch of half-penny periodicals by Alfred Harmsworth and, more importantly, by the birth of *Comic Cuts* and *Illustrated Chips*. Despite being considerably less sensational, these publications became popular very quickly, and according to Murray, '[lead] to Harmsworth setting up Amalgamated Press in 1901' (2017: 45). As in the case of many American publishing houses in the 1930s and 1940s, AP had a 'house style'; similar to the works of Töpffer, and images were accompanied by text positioned underneath. Murray describes this as 'a style that defined British comics for decades' (2017: 45).

On both sides of the Atlantic, comic strips in newspapers remained popular, despite the increasing importance of advertising revenue, which diminished the space available for comics within the papers themselves. It was a logical progression for publishers to move the strips from within the papers to separate publications, which additionally offered opportunities for advertising revenue of their own. In the US, this happened in 1933, with the publication of *Famous Funnies*, a collection of reprinted strips that had previously featured in newspapers. Although comic books in the form of a bound magazine are sometimes thought to be an American invention, this is simply not true. By 1933, comics were being published in bound form across the world, as we will see in Chapter 3; and although the US was not the first country where comics appeared as separate publications, it certainly did become one of the most influential, in part due to the fact that printing technologies were more advanced, meaning that comics could be produced cheaper, faster, and to a higher quality. These new 'comic books' quickly outstripped the popularity of their newspaper equivalents and publishers continually required new material in order to satisfy the appetites of the readers: Ron Goulart calls this 'the cornerstone for one of the most lucrative branches of magazine publishing' (2007: 163). The success of *Famous Funnies* led to the creation of more publishers for these new stand-alone comics. Moving comics out of the newspapers led to an increase in younger readers, who were not typically buying daily newspapers in large numbers but did begin to buy comic books. Rather than reading the funny pages of their parents' choice of newspaper, younger readers were free to choose their own reading material and pick their favourite strips and characters.

It was at this point that the first superheroes appeared on American newsstands, starting with Superman in *Action Comics #1* in 1938. The world was on the cusp of the Second World War; the appearance of superheroes was not a coincidence. There is a good deal of politics and nationalism bound up in these early comic characters. Superman has the dubious distinction of being both a nationalist figure and an immigrant since he was both an American *and* an alien from the Planet Krypton, who was created by two first-generation Jewish immigrants to the US. When Captain America first appeared in 1941, immediately before the entry of the US into the Second World War, he was punching Hitler squarely on the jaw. Captain America's creator, Joe Simon, asserted that the character was a 'consciously political creation as [Jack Kirby and I] felt war was inevitable: The opponents to the war were all quite well organized. We wanted to have our say too' (Kirby, qtd in Wright, 2003: 26). The superhero was a very popular figure during the war years, and being able to manipulate the events of the war in favour of a US victory made for compelling storylines, and the mixture of patriotism and nationalism that the characters displayed worked well as a boost to national morale. The comics were aimed at younger readers initially, and their readership grew with their popularity; indeed, at their height, some comics series were selling a million copies per issue. Such publications, often collectively referred to as 'the mainstream', were produced by teams of artists, working to strict time and creative constraints. There was very little room for artistic freedom, and for the few publishers of this era that are still operating (notably Marvel and DC), these constraints remain and the publishers employ a consistent 'house style'.

Of course, the 'mainstream' was not confined to superheroes but spanned the whole spectrum of genres. Newsstands groaned under the weight of every kind of comic book, from romance and 'girl's comics' to superheroes, to horror and crime. Fingeroth writes, 'by the early 1950s, the superhero comics fad was pretty much dead [in the US]. DC Comics published Superman, Batman and Wonder Woman, but that was all. The genre that sold in huge numbers was horror' (2008: 14). However, something was on the horizon that would put superheroes back into the spotlight. Although the popularity of comics, especially with younger readers, increased, they were less popular with those who believed that children were being corrupted by their reading material. In many ways, the same arguments that are levelled against television and video games today were in use against Comics in the 1940s and 1950s. In 1954, psychiatrist Fredric Wertham published *Seduction of the Innocent*, whose influence is still felt in the Comics world today. According to Wertham, comic books were one of the main causes of juvenile delinquency. There is no evidence that children who read comics are at risk of any ill effect whatsoever and Wertham does not provide examples of children suffering from the effects of reading comics. Although we would now dismiss these arguments, by 1950s standards they were persuasive, and the objections of Wertham and his supporters led to the 1953 *United States Senate Subcommittee on Juvenile Delinquency*; the result of the subcommittee was self-regulation within the industry in the shape of the 1954 Comic Magazine Association of America (CMAA) and the Comics Code Authority (CCA), and newsstands were only allowed to stock comics that bore the distinctive CCA stamp. The regulations that the CCA championed effectively put an end to horror publications, leading to a renaissance of superheroes. It is important to note that the CCA was not necessarily compulsory but its far-reaching influence led to negative results for those who dared to defy it. It was officially retired in 2011, by which time only a few publishers were still following its guidelines and the CCA itself had very little power over the publication and distribution of comics.

The UK market comprised a narrower range of themes and target audiences, with the majority of titles aimed at young readers. Adventure comics were popular, as were publications such as *The Dandy* (launched 1937) and *The Beano* (launched 1938), both published by Dundee-based DC Thomson. These comics differed from earlier offerings, especially those by Amalgamated Press, in their style and characters. Rather than keeping the text separate from the image, both comics used bubbles and captions in the same way as American mainstream publications and most modern comics. The majority of the characters were working class, living in situations that would be recognisable to the readership; the exceptions to this are characters such as Lord Snooty and his Pals (featured in *The Beano*), who typify a very British stereotype of the upper classes. Despite the class differences between Lord Snooty and the working-class characters such as the Bash Street Kids (*The Beano*), they are all children, attending school and engaging in typical childhood behaviours and activities. This stood in stark contrast to the majority of American comics, which featured adult characters. Most superhero characters were adults, and teenage characters did not become common in the American mainstream until the creation of Spiderman in 1962; though some story arcs did show 'origin' narratives of a character's childhood, this was not common.

In the 1950s, American crime and horror comics were introduced to the UK and, as had already happened in the US, this caused a moral panic. Not only were American comics being sold, but British publishers were also creating their own versions of famous titles such as *Tales from the Crypt* and *The Vault of Horror*. In November 1954, a reporter for *The Times* wrote: 'The problem which now faces society in the trade that has sprung up of presenting sadism, crime, lust, physical monstrosity, and horror to the young is an urgent and a grave one' (qtd in Springhall, 1999: 142). The subsequent campaign against the sale of these comics was headed by Geoffrey Fisher, the Archbishop of Canterbury, and in 1955, the Parliament passed the Children and Young Persons (Harmful Publications) Act. Though nowhere near as restrictive as the guidelines of the CCA, this act severely limited the types of comics that could be sold. In contrast to the changes that occurred after similar measures in the US, the UK market did not change drastically. In the 1950s and 1960s, the most popular children's comics remained available and very popular, with a large proportion of the market share going to *The Beano*, *The Dandy,* and *The Eagle* (1950–1969). Despite its modest tenure in comparison to other British comics, *The Eagle* was extremely popular. It was conceived and launched by Anglican vicar Marcus Morris who wanted to create an adventure comic that was 'decent' and educational, but also fun and thrilling. The star of the stories was Dan Dare, a pilot and adventurer, though the initial suggestion was for a priest called 'Lex Christian'. It is not difficult to see why this decision was changed early in the development stages. *The Eagle* was successful in being a wholesome, yet fun comic and the first issue sold 900,000 copies (Sabin, 1993). By the time it ceased publication, in 1969, circulation had dwindled but the market was still relatively buoyant. The sister comic of *The Eagle* was *Girl*, with a modest tenure from 1951 to 1964, also founded by the Rev Morris. Most of the stories featured wholesome female protagonists involved in minor scrapes but always remaining morally upright. Girls' comics were very successful during this period. The longest running of this type is *Bunty*, which ran from 1958 to 2001 and contained similar stories to *Girl*, mostly set in schools and dealing with female friendship. However, the Anglophone market on both sides of the Atlantic was on the brink of a change that came from below.

Rebel readers: comics go underground

Restrictions put in place by the CCA and the Children and Young Persons (Harmful Publications) Act may have fundamentally changed the shape and focus of the mainstream Comics industry in the US and UK, changing the offerings available at newsstands, but these restrictions did not reach all of Comics. If anything, they forced the creation of a fertile space for the growth of a wealth of rebellious, obscene, politically charged and technically innovative comics, free from the constraints of publishers' rules and demands. Mainstream publishing houses had, and still have, 'house guidelines' governing the development of every comic, with restrictions brought into force at every stage of creation and publication. The freedom allowed to 'underground' artists by these independent models has been, in part, a major influence on the diversity of story, theme, and art that is a key feature of the modern form. As early as the late 1920s, anonymous artists had been producing pornographic comic books featuring popular characters, especially Betty Boop, as well as celebrities, such as Mae West or Clark Gable, produced without copyright permission and disseminated through adult shops. These small books became known as 'Tijuana Bibles', designed to give the impression that they were manufactured and smuggled into the US from Tijuana, Mexico, and these are often considered the parents of the underground Comics (or 'Comix') scene. Unlike many of the other comic books available at the time that collected strips from newspapers and republished them, Tijuana Bibles featured original material. They were printed cheaply and quickly on poor quality paper, sold for 20 or 25 cents in barber shops, bars, tobacconists, and similar places. Though their popularity dwindled after the Second World War, as pornography became more easily available, Tijuana Bibles demonstrated how Comics could easily and successfully take advantage of a commercial infrastructure *not* related to the mainstream Comics industry for distribution and, moreover, they confirmed that there was definitely a market for such publications. As Danny Fingeroth writes, 'the underground Comix were about as far from the mainstream as it was possible to be... that was the whole point' (2008: 17). Edward Shannon suggests that, 'in retrospect, underground comix seem a natural product of drug-fuelled 1960s rebellion, but early in the decade there would seem to have been little appetite for such work in an America that defined comic books in terms of Mickey Mouse and Superman' (2012: 629).

The birth of underground Comix took time. The first underground strip was *The Adventures of Jesus*, created by Frank Stack, under the *nom-de-plume* 'Foolbert Sturgeon', first published in 1962. The series followed Jesus, who arrives on Earth in the late twentieth century to a world that is beyond help, jaded, and decrepit. It is darkly funny and witty, with much of the iconoclasm, subversiveness, and irreverence that would become typical of the underground. By the late 1960s, such strips became both regular and frequent. Many of the earliest of these publications were created for friends of the artist; others appeared in underground and university newspapers. As I mentioned in Chapter 1, the 'x' was meant to denote the 'X-rated', signalling that these publications were not for children, and distinguishing them from the mainstream. Roy Cook writes:

In crossing boundaries and breaking taboos, the (white, male) underground seemed all too willing to depict rape, violence, misogyny, and racial stereotypes, often in a seemingly positive, (or at least non-critical) light. Such content was celebrated within the underground comics solely for its transgressive nature, regardless of whether it was being mobilised toward any larger positive message, moral, or meaning.

(2017: 36)

Many underground artists did use their work to make statements, especially political ones, although they are not always positive. Denis Kitchen describes underground comix as 'the bastard child of a wayward generation'. He adds, 'As someone who was there near the very beginning, I can say with certainty that there was no grand conspiracy, no secret cell activity and no intellectual summit' (Skinn, 2004: 6). They were not an isolated invention, as much as a logical continuation of the rebellious spirit of the 1960s: 'When the beatnik and mod eras mutated into the hippie movement, and the new establishment became vilified through its politics and policing of such, equally new models were needed. Rebels, with a cause' (2004: 10). In the light of this it seems appropriate that Robert Crumb's *Zap Comix* (accompanied by the tagline 'The comic that plugs you in!!') was first published in 1967, the year of the famous Summer of Love in the US. The counterculture movement and the anti-war crusade intensified during this period, as a direct response to the Vietnam War. In this political climate, underground comix found their niche as a vehicle for stories about drug use, sexual freedom, political unrest, social rebellion, and violence, all of which were largely absent in the mainstream. In both the US and the UK, these books were sold in 'head shops', which Roger Sabin describes as 'hippie shops that sold fashionable clothing, joss-sticks, drug paraphernalia, and so on' (1993: 45). Sabin furthers the link to hippie and drug culture by pointing out that many of the cover designs imitated LSD-inspired artwork to increase sales.

The influence of Robert Crumb on the underground movement cannot be overstated. He started out as an artist for a greetings card company after leaving high school. He drew comics on the side and, after leaving his greeting card job, became part of a group of young artists involved in producing comics within the San Francisco Bay Area, the epicentre of underground comix in the late-1960s. In many ways, Crumb's work epitomises the Summer of Love and the counterculture movement. He took LSD (which was still legal at the time) and his characters were inspired by his many drug trips. His best-known characters include Angelfood McSpade, a grotesque racist depiction of a black African woman, with obscenely large breasts and buttocks, who speaks in 'jive' (a form of African American vernacular English that was associated with Harlem) and is sexually promiscuous; Fritz the Cat, an amoral con artist, whose frequent adventures almost always involved sex; and Mr Natural, a bald, bearded old man who is both a guru and a hedonist. Crumb included himself in many of his comics as a sex-obsessed, self-hating pseudo-intellectual, basking in his 'resolutely countercultural […] jaundiced view of America, […] sexual mores, and […] himself' (Contemporary Authors Online, 2013: n.p.).

Shannon describes Crumb's comics as 'a flood from a burst dam, detailing what is not right with his mind in excruciating detail – and overtly political terms' (2012: 629); and they are a mixture of politics, autobiography, and hippie culture. For Crumb, the attraction of comix was their freedom from censorship:

> People forget that that was what it was all about. That was why we did it. We didn't have anybody standing over us saying 'No, you can't draw this' or 'You can't show that'. We could do whatever we wanted.
>
> (Crumb in Sabin, 1996: 95)

Crumb's influence is undeniable, and he had a dedicated following of young cartoonists who imitated his style but nonetheless, his work generated considerable controversy. His views on women, especially, have been the target of criticism, since much of his work focuses on graphic depictions of sexual violence and the abuse of women. Fellow underground comix artist, Trina Robbins, said, 'It's weird to me how willing people are to overlook the hideous darkness in Crumb's work… What the hell is funny about rape and murder?' (qtd in Sabin, 1996: 92).

Robbins' point is valid; nothing is funny about either of these topics, but their pervasiveness in the male–dominated comix world led to an overabundance of misogynist works. The same rebellious spirit that drove male artists also drove their female counterparts who succeeded in attracting the political and social backing of the women's liberation movements during the late-1960s and 1970s. In 1970, Robbins edited the first all-female underground comix work, *It Ain't Me, Babe,* followed in 1972 by *Wimmen's Comix* (founded by Patricia Moodian and the newly formed Women's Comix Collective) and *Tits & Clits* (edited by Joyce Farmer and Lyn Chevely). The Women's Comix Collective was not without its own problems. The Collective was very much opposed to the publications of male artists, notably Crumb, and the presence of his partner Aline Kominsky-Crumb in the group led to a rift in 1975. Kominsky-Crumb's presence in a staunchly feminist organisation while also being married to their 'nemesis' raises a series of questions. For example, does Aline's conjugal relationship to Crumb negate her membership of such a group? Can one be married to a man who was frequently identified as a 'sexist pig' while proudly wearing the 'feminist' label? Kominsky-Crumb's work followed many of the same themes as her husband's, but as a woman she maintained an independent stance of her own. One of her first works, the semi-autobiographical 'Goldie', is an 'unflinching, and unglamorous, depiction of sexuality' (Chute, 2010: 21). The young Goldie is shown masturbating and exploring her burgeoning sexuality. Hillary Chute makes the following observation about the public response to Kominsky-Crumb's work compared to that of her husband: 'her underwhelming reception contrasts markedly to that of her husband, cartoonist Robert Crumb, who has been canonised exactly for writing the darker side of (his own) tortured male sexuality' (Chute, 2010: 31).

Despite many controversies, the underground allowed artists a freedom not offered by big publishers in much the same way that digital and web comics do. Many anthologies parodied long-established mainstream genres; for example, *Young*

Lust (1970–1993), which featured work by Bill Griffith and Art Spiegelman, were spoofs of 1950s romance comics, and *Bizarre Sex* (1972–1982) was influenced by sci-fi, featuring art by Richard 'Grass' Green, one of the few African American creators. Perhaps the most topical for today's audience was *Slow Death* (1970–1992), focussed on corporate pollution, toxic waste, and environmentalism. As we have already seen in the autobiographical works of Aline Kominsky-Crumb and her husband, the underground gave artists the freedom to write and draw their own lives.

A key publication in the British underground is *Viz* (1979–present). Founded by Chris Donald, who initially produced the comic in his bedroom, *Viz* epitomises the ethos of the underground movement. The first issue was sold at punk gigs in the North East of England and circulation grew steadily to around 5,000 in the early 1980s, peaking at over 1 million by the early 1990s. Currently, *Viz* retains its place in British popular culture as an adult comic with many long-running jokes and characters, and an average circulation of 45,000. One such character is 'Roger Mellie – the Man on the Telly', a parody of David Frost. Mellie is a misogynist television presenter whose catchphrase is 'Hello, good evening and bollocks!' Another long-running character is Sid the Sexist, a man who is unable to talk to women and resorts to crude, sexist humour, usually resulting in him having objects inserted into his bottom by disgusted women. Both Roger and Sid are clear examples of the type of humour that *Viz* favours and part of the reason for its longevity.

Justin Green's *Binky Brown Meets the Holy Virgin Mary* (1972) is a landmark text in both underground comix and autographics (the collective term for autobiography and life writing in the Comics form that I will consider in more detail in Chapter 6). Green had previously been published in several anthologies before beginning work on *Binky Brown*. The book follows Green's avatar, Binky, and his struggle with a form of Obsessive-Compulsive Disorder (OCD) that is religiously focussed, against a background of a Catholic childhood in 1950s Chicago. Binky is raised and educated as a Catholic, forming an image of God that exacerbates his feelings of guilt and provides the framework for his OCD symptoms. The book is unflinching and deeply unsettling in its honesty. Chute sees the work as 'delv[ing] into and forcefully pictur[ing] non-normative sexuality'; she adds that *Binky Brown* is a graphic novel since 'the quality of work, its approach, parameters, and sensibility [denote a] seriousness of purpose' (2010: 19, 17). The influence of *Binky Brown* is very far-reaching indeed, and those who cite it as an influence include Aline Kominsky-Crumb, Robert Crumb, Howard Cruse, and, famously, Art Spiegelman. Spiegelman stated that 'without *Binky Brown* there would be no *Maus*' (1995: 4). This positive endorsement points to the start of new era of Comics history: the rise of the graphic novel and the advent of the modern comic book.

The gates are open: comics everywhere

One of the most famous graphic novels of the modern era began as three pages in an underground anthology in 1972. At the request of Justin Green, Art Spiegelman drew a short comic about his father's experience of the Shoah; it was published in *Funny Aminals #1* and, with that, the groundwork was laid for *Maus*. First serialised from 1980 to 1991 in *Raw*, a magazine published by Spiegelman and his wife, Françoise Mouly, the graphic novel format with which we are now familiar appeared in 1986 in a collected volume that contained the first half of the total comic; the second half was published in 1991. The publication of *Maus* caused a stir in the literary world: here was a work that was distinctly *not* literature but that commanded a level of respect not yet awarded to Comics. *The New York Times* curiously wrote that 'Art Spiegelman doesn't draw comic books', presumably intending this as a compliment (qtd in Witek, 2004: n.p.). The Pulitzer Prize Committee awarded *Maus* a Special Award in Letters in 1992. Since then, Spiegelman's book has remained at the top of any list of 'great' Comics and is regularly included on reading lists in universities and high schools; collections of academic essays and conferences are dedicated to *Maus,* and it is often treated with a near hagiolatrous fervour. Many artists cite Spiegelman as a primary influence on their works, including Marjane Satrapi's *Persepolis* (2000) and Alison Bechdel's *Fun Home*

(2006), as well as the works of Chris Ware and Craig Thompson. It is undoubtedly an important text and predecessor to many later works of autobiography as we shall see later in Chapter 6.

However, though Maus initiated a debate in relation to the legitimacy of Comics and is often regarded as the text responsible for the rise of the graphic novel, this claim is not strictly accurate. There are two issues to consider here. Firstly, we need to realise that Comics did not suddenly *become* a legitimate form for telling significant stories, even though *Maus* was an important milestone in their *recognition* as a valid cultural form. We need to recall that the genesis of the form itself ranges from Hogarth's moralising to Krazy Kat's modernist surrealism to the sexual honesty of the underground. In this context, *Maus* did not change what Comics had achieved but it did help to change the public perception of the form's potential. Secondly, *Maus* did not exist in a vacuum, nor was it the only text that was breaking new ground in the mid-1980s. The year 1986 saw the publication of two other highly influential works alongside *Maus*: Alan Moore and Dave Gibbons' *Watchmen,* which was a dystopian science-fiction-meets-superheroes horror story that presented an alternative narrative of the Cold War, in which America was victorious in Vietnam and Nixon remained in power until 1985. Moore and Gibbons used their book to deconstruct and problematise the superhero narrative. Frank Miller's *The Dark Knight Returns* pursued a similar trajectory, taking the superhero story and complicating it. Miller's Batman is ageing and disillusioned and the book frames the character in a far darker way than previously seen. These three comics were distinctly adult publications, despite using genres that were typically suitable for children, and they signalled the arrival of the modern era.

It is important to note that all three comics, now considered graphic novels, were not originally published in their current formats. They were all published as a weekly series initially (*Watchmen* consists of twelve parts, *The Dark Knight Returns* four, and *Maus* eleven) and were collected into bound volumes only at a later stage. Although these books may come under the heading of 'trade paperbacks', a name that is sometimes given to long-form comic books that collect together previous series runs, it is important to recognise that trade paperbacks of this kind are different from graphic novels. By twenty-first century standards, a typical graphic novel would not be sold as issues, but only as a single bound book. Trade paperbacks proved to be an excellent strategy for publishers to adopt, and they sold well. Mainstream series that had begun to sell badly moved from single issues to trade paperbacks in order to revitalise sales, not only in specialist comics shops but also in bookshops. This strategy allowed Comics to take its place as a form of storytelling for readers of all ages and interests, but it was not without consequences. The move to the high street bookshop meant that Comics could now be considered as 'literature' and that those works that made it onto bookshelves began to attract the critical attention of literary reviewers. *Maus* won the Pulitzer Prize in 1992; *Watchmen* was the only comic to appear on *Time's* 2005 'All-Time 100 Greatest Novels' list; *Fun Home* was a finalist for the 2006 National Book Critics Circle Award; and *Persepolis* ranked #5 on *Newsweek's* list of the ten best fiction books of the decade. It is important to note that *Persepolis* is not fiction but autobiography, since in it artist Marjane Satrapi tells the story of her childhood in Iran during and after the Islamic Revolution in 1979. This mislabelling of key and popular texts is a recurring issue with graphic novels that are also non-fiction; the connotations of 'novel' are strong enough to override any suggestion of the word's non-fiction classification. I have already discussed the non-literary identity of Comics in Chapter 1; such praise for these comics is both well-deserved (as they are often beautifully constructed) and problematic (because this praise seeks to play down the fact that they are Comics and instead compare them to something 'more worthy').

At the same time, the American market was in the grip of the 'British Invasion', a term that refers specifically to a small group of British writers and artists whose popularity grew in the late 1980s while they were being employed in the production of American titles. The most prominent included writers such as Alan Moore, Neil Gaiman, and Grant Morrison, as well as artists Brian Bolland and Dave Gibbons who had all been previously employed in the production of the British anthology series *2000 AD*. They then moved to the US to work for DC Comics.

According to Douglas Wolk, the catalyst for the invasion was Alan Moore's *Swamp Thing* (1983):

> His commercial breakthrough came in 1983, when he took over *Saga of the Swamp Thing*, a terrible American comic book; Moore took the opportunity to show off the range of his technique, which resulted in a certain amount of purple prose ('Clouds like plugs of bloodied cotton wool dab ineffectually at the slashed wrists of the sky') and a lot of thrilling formal experiments that had never been tried in mainstream comics before. His success led directly to American comics' 'British invasion'.
>
> (2003: n.p.)

Wolk goes on to explain that the selling point of Moore's work was his position as 'arguably the first [of] mainstream writers who seemed fully in command of his style', and consequently, 'other writers, mostly British, started to follow his example of sensitivity to language' (2007: 27). Prior to this, 'the actual text in American comic books was generally pretty impoverished until the '80s [and it had] always been subordinate to the plot and storytelling' (Wolk: 2007: 26). The 'invasion' that was attributed to Moore provided the impetus for a new imprint, *Vertigo*, in 1993; the aim was to target a more mature audience and provide an outlet for more violent, adult works.

Many artists and writers had become so well-known to their readers in the 1940s and 1950s that they could be identified by their individual styles. By the 1990s, some artists and writers were becoming known beyond the Comics community and their work was recognisable to the general public. Some writers, such as Neil Gaiman, had also become successful novelists. Others, like Frank Miller, took their work to Hollywood and were involved in the transfer of their comics from page to screen. In some cases, things also worked the other way around. For example, Michael Chabon's novel *The Amazing Adventures of Kavalier and Clay*, which retold the history of the Golden Age of the superhero, won the Pulitzer Prize in 2001; Chabon then went on to write for DC and Dark Horse. Jonathan Lethem, whose novels play with genre conventions, resurrected a long-defunct Marvel character, Omega the Unknown, and the resulting series was published in ten issues in 2007, before being collected together in 2008. However, the seeming fluidity of the borders between Literature and Comics shown in the careers of these writers is insufficient to support the claim that Comics has become a subset of the category of Literature. It is possible to identify similar crossovers between Literature and Film as in the cases of authors John Irving or William Goldman, who are also successful screenwriters. It is this fluidity that is an important part of the modern Comics industry, especially in relation to what we may call 'crossover media' (see Chapter 4). Just as film adaptations of novels are now common, so do comics adaptations of both films and novels that now exist. There are comics adaptations of every conceivable text, from the literary classics (*Jane Eyre* by Charlotte Brontë or Mary Shelley's *Frankenstein*) to science fiction (Octavia Butler's *Kindred*) to the *Diary of Anne Frank* or the plays of Shakespeare. The modern Comics world is diverse, inclusive, and accessible. Comics is still a popular form, as were the proto-comics of thousands of years ago, though the journey to public acceptance has been long, complex, and circuitous.

3   Going global

Comics on the world stage

Comics is an international form that exists in virtually every society and cultural milieu across the globe. The histories and development of each national or linguistic Comics tradition interconnect with, and complement, each other as international developments in printing and publication technologies began to exert pressure on particular aspects of the production and marketing of comics. As we saw in Chapter 2, Comics history is distinct from that of other narrative forms and their origins. The novel, for example, grew out of eighteenth-century northern European realism, finding an early text in *Robinson Crusoe* (1719). In his book *The Rise of the Novel*, Ian Watt discusses the ways in which the novel was influenced by a change in the composition of Defoe's readership as a result of the rise of economic individualism (1957: 60). At its origin, many novels were concerned with both realist representation of quotidian reality and how this new literary form can influence national identity construction and nation-building (see Anderson, 1983). It is a form that is intrinsically linked to the political and social constructions of northern Europe. Comics does not have the same history. This chapter will discuss the histories and concerns of comics across the world.

While comics in North America were taking the newsstands by storm, or generating political discussion in the UK, they were having similar far-reaching effects in countries across the world. Federico Zanettin writes that 'most if not all European countries had a tradition of printed visual art' (2008: 2); we can add that a large number of countries throughout the rest of the world also developed these traditions, with those in East Asia achieving special prominence. The focus of this chapter will be twofold: to discuss Comics as an international form, with an emphasis on key issues raised by internationalisation, and to consider specific non-Anglophone Comics traditions, their histories, developments, and current international positions. In the first section, I examine the developments that have been brought about by changes in publication, printing technologies, and practices of dissemination: issues such as how these changes have affected the types of comics that are released, how they are consumed, and by whom? I also ask: what questions are raised by translating a comic from one language to another? And what additional problems are raised by the translation of images? How do we translate images and, by extension, cultures, where the representations themselves have a specific meaning for a particular culture? The second part of this chapter complements Chapter 2's Anglophone-focussed histories of Comics, shifting attention to some of the most influential and popular non-Anglophone Comics cultures and traditions. Attention will be given to Japanese comics (*Manga,* 漫画) and Franco-Belgian comics (*Bandes Dessinées*), and also to Comics in Italy (*Fumetti*), Spain (*Historietas*), India, and Korea (*Manhwa,* 만화 or 漫畫).

Comics and the global village

The term 'global village' was coined by Canadian media theorist Marshall McLuhan in the 1960s. At the time, it denoted the daily creation, transmission, and consumption of media directed at global audiences who, by virtue of television, could be accessed electronically, but this has now emerged as 'the dominant term for expressing a global coexistence altered by transnational commerce, migration, and culture' (Lee, qtd in Ryan, 2012: 160). In the twenty-first century, most people do not think it is unusual to be exposed to a range of media from around the world, some of it with accompanying subtitles or dubbing, alongside local media forms. It is both typical and expected for recipients to enjoy American, Asian, and European media often without consciously recognising the jumps in comprehension that are needed to move between them. A *Manga* fan may adapt with ease to the right-to-left reading style of Japanese comics, before moving back to Western left-to-right reading style.

This sharing of works has a long history. There had been some international transmission of proto-comics, but the practice of borrowing across language barriers accelerated with the advent of *fin de siècle* newspaper strips. For example, *Histoire de M. Vieux Bois*, Rodolphe Töpffer's most famous work, had been published in several languages across Europe in 1837; an English version was published in Britain in 1841 and in America a year later. Similarly, the American strip *The Katzenjammer Kids* (1897–2006) borrowed heavily from Wilhelm Busch's *Max und Moritz* (1865), originally published in Germany (see Chapter 2). By the 1930s, imports of American mainstream comics into France and Belgium had become commonplace, though, as Sabin observes, this ceased 'during the war years due to the German occupation and consequent banning of imports from America' (Sabin, 1993: 283). Sabin adds that the 'isolationism from American material [caused by the ban] was not necessarily duplicated in other parts of Europe. In Germany, for example, American comics were common, with original material often entering the country post-1945 via the military bases' (1993: 283). In the twenty-first century, the range of publication models available for comics, discussed in more detail in Chapter 4, has meant that more texts are available to a much wider selection of readers, with the result that not only are texts available in their original languages, but that there is also a greater likelihood that they will appear translated.

The international distribution and sharing of comics has both positive and negative consequences. It is difficult to regard the widespread sale of, engagement with, and enjoyment of any narrative form negatively. Indeed, the international expansion of Comics industries means that the diversity of texts available in any particular country or language has increased exponentially. Not only does this mean a wider choice for 'omnivorous' readers who are likely to enjoy a varied range of comics, but it also engages those readers who may otherwise restrict their reading to a very specific genre, artist type, or distinctive style. The result is, therefore, an advantage not only for the reader, but also for the creator. For the creator, it means a significantly increased readership and potentially greater recognition beyond their home country and native language. In addition to the increase of numbers of readers, the boost in interest has helped to generate new ways of disseminating independent creations; this is most obvious in the rise of web comics that are shared via social media or dedicated Comics portals (see Chapter 1). There is also, however, a downside to this increased readership and distribution. Some creators will always be more popular than others, and this can lead to certain creators receiving most of the interest, to the detriment of others. Publishers that have a larger budget for translation and localisation are also likely to overshadow smaller companies, especially independent small presses. When one type or publisher of Comics becomes the 'norm', it can erase the linguistic or cultural nuances characteristic of local creators, especially if the publisher has a 'house style' to which all artists must adhere.

Though we may be comfortable with discussion of any art within its specific critical and cultural environment, it is crucial to remember that art is not made in isolation; it is made within communities in which ideas, inspirations, themes, and techniques can grow and develop. Though artists may work individually, they exist within a wider community, and their work is likely to draw on the culture from which it comes. Artists working in any form will observe what their peers are doing and, given the different elements that comprise the Comics form, will collaborate with each other. At its extreme, and in societies that protect intellectual property by law, this might involve plagiarism, but in a collegial form in which different talents can combine, but it might be a normal part of the way through which art and narrative can grow. With the increasing internationalisation of Comics, the easy dissemination of works and ideas via the internet and the constant exchange of media across linguistic and cultural borders, artists can be exposed to a wide selection of influences. This cross-fertilisation is an important part of the enduring health of a narrative form. The different types of sharing and cross-fertilisation generally relate to the appropriation of existing artistic styles commonly associated with one cultural or national tradition being taken wholesale into another in order to innovate or de-familiarise an already familiar narrative, or simply to reinvigorate the assumptions and 'norms' of an existing art style. There are two related examples worth considering in this context: the *Manga Shakespeare* series by Richard Appignanesi and various artists (2005–2009) and Kei Ishiyama's *Grimm Manga Tales* (2012).

The *Manga Shakespeare* series was launched by Self-Made Hero, a British publisher, in 2005. Fourteen of Shakespeare's plays have been adapted by Richard Appignanesi and drawn by artists from various artistic backgrounds. The title *Manga* is curious here. As I discuss later in this chapter, *Manga* is the name given to Japanese language comics and translations thereof; the term is also used for texts that use the artistic and narrative style of Japanese works. In the case of this example, the texts are in English, and *Manga* is used to describe the art style that it employs. In addition, the books read left-to-write, which is not the norm in *Manga*. In her article on the series, Yukari Yoshihara writes that the publishers 'decided to employ *Manga* artists residing in the UK [to] help cultivate local *Manga* talents' (2016: 114). While many of these artists are Japanese and originally worked as *Mangaka* (*Manga* creators) in Japan, some had only worked in the UK. In this case, the word is being used to suggest that it is drawn in a style that is reminiscent of *Manga*, but not a strict imitation of it. This example draws together a canonical figure such as Shakespeare and 'translates' a text into the *Manga* style. We may see this as an example of cultural capital. According to sociologist Pierre Bourdieu, cultural capital is the collection of educational, intellectual, and symbolic elements of an individual that are acquired through belonging to a certain social class. People of higher social status will have higher cultural capital, as some forms are valued over others and can further social mobility (1986: 241–258). As Shakespeare's works are considered highbrow, they command a high level of cultural capital. While in the UK, *Manga* does not necessarily have a high level of cultural capital, it certainly does in Japan. Yoshihara writes that 'the globalized/localized cultural capital of manga is combined with the cultural mega-capital of

Shakespeare, which has likewise become globally shared and localized' (2016: 114).

Discussion of the *Manga Shakespeare* is complicated by the fact that the publisher, writer, and many of the artists are not Japanese by nationality or artistic training. Rather than this being a 'true' coming-together of two cultures, it is heavily mediated through the lens of a target culture and the desire to appropriate an established form. According to Joe Keener:

> The motivation behind these phenomena is not just an attempt to emulate a financially successful form of Japanese popular culture, but to appropriate some of the soft power that Japan has accrued through the almost worldwide success of its manga. Soft power is the ability to get what one wants through attraction, and Japanese manga's infiltrating of not just western cultural products but imaginations confer soft power on Japan.
>
> (2015: 43)

The *Manga Shakespeare* series aims to make a canonical writer of high cultural status accessible to new and younger readers through a popular cultural form. For Iulia Drăghici, 'in reading Manga Shakespeare, one can come across a lively interchange between high and pop culture that captivates the reader, brightening up the sometimes equivocal cultural site of meaning that we call Shakespeare' (2015: 117). This 'lively interchange' is not simply the fusion of high and popular culture (Shakespeare wrote, after all, for the masses) but also the amalgamation of two important and culturally significant narrative art forms from two distinct geographical locations. Or, to put the matter a little differently, the texts of a writer who already has a global reputation, notwithstanding Drăghici's comment, are aligned with a Japanese popular form to produce something that exceeds the national contexts within which they were originally generated.

Japanese *Mangaka* Kei Ishiyama's *Grimm Manga Tales* (2007) stands in contrast to the *Manga Shakespeare* series. It is published in two volumes, and consists of a range of stories from another canonical writer usually associated with children's stories, *Grimm's Fairy Tales*: 'Little Red Riding Hood', 'Rapunzel', 'Hänsel and Gretel', 'The Two Brothers', 'The Twelve Hunters', 'Snow White', 'The Frog King', 'Puss in Boots', and 'The Singing, Springing Lark'. The most obvious thing to note from this list is that these stories are northern European in origin, and were first made available in print through the collections of Jacob and Wilhelm Grimm. They are a quintessential part of European folklore, and their narrative elements are dependent on their environment and culture. On the surface, it may seem that Ishiyama's *Grimm Manga Tales* is a fusion of Western narratives and Eastern artistic styles in a way that the *Manga Shakespeare* series is not. *Grimm Manga Tales* is an 'OEL', an 'Original English Language' *Manga*, and published by Tokyopop, an American publisher. It therefore straddles the Western/Eastern split, albeit in a different way to *Manga Shakespeare*: Appignanesi's series uses Western narratives and artists, publishing in a clearly Western model, but using Eastern artistic tradition to bring something new to the story whereas Ishiyama's series uses equally Western narratives, but represented through the lens of Japanese creative strategies. This type of cultural exchange is occurring at different levels across different cultural and linguistic borders, creating what we may variously refer to as a 'globalised mediascape' (MacWilliams, 2008: 12) or, less encouragingly, a 'Gordian knot of transnational cultural flows' (Leheny, 2006: 233).

The problem of translation

With an ever-shrinking world and increasing international demand for comics, it is necessary to consider translation, and especially how and why specific comics or collections migrate between languages. Translators and translation theorists regularly debate the different approaches that can be taken in the activity of translating any text. Most agree, however, that the aim of translation is to move beyond words and into the realm of cultural signs and understanding. Weissbort and Eysteinsson argue that we understand other places and cultures 'by building linguistic bridges across the channels that divide language spheres and cultural regions, whether by the rewriting of messages and works in another tongue, or through other interventions by individuals who possess knowledge in more than one language' (2006: 1). They go on to suggest that

> [L]iterary translation [...] draws on experience from diverse fields of human experience. Literature combines cultural and aesthetic values, and this makes its translation so difficult and challenging, but also so urgent. [...] Literary texts of course also demand particular attention to language itself, its resonances and references, its historical depth as well as its personal relevance, and this gives an extra dimension to the 'problem' of the translation.
>
> (2006: 2, 3)

If the structure, language games, and referential nature of text-based narratives demand extra attention when it comes to translation, then Comics require a further consideration: the meaning and status of the image. It is important to remember, as Altenberg and Owen write, that there is 'no single history of comics translation, but rather many national and formal and thematic histories' (2015: iv). As such we cannot create a universal holistic history of translation so we 'need to begin with small clusters of individual translations' (2015: iv).

There are two components to Comics translation: verbal translation and image/sign translation. It is not enough to translate the textual components of the comic (the speech bubbles and captions), but the images themselves are part of a language system that needs to be considered within its cultural, national, and representational contexts. In some cases, the translation involves replacing one textual component in the source language with another in the target language where there is an exact equivalent. It should be noted that this also includes onomatopoeia such as 'splash' (falling into a French river will lead to 'plouf', while this will be rendered as 'platsch' in German) or animal sounds (English dogs say 'woof'; Spanish dogs say 'guau'; Korean dogs say 'meong'). Zanettin compares this to software localisation, the process whereby a piece of computer software is adapted to a new culture that would include language translation, measurements, currency, and date formats. He adds:

> Most 'grammatical devices' such as speech balloons, ono-matopoeia and visual metaphors are used in comics produced in many different cultures and can be seen as central to comics as an art form, while other features are perhaps less salient. However, there is not one single 'language' of comics, as each regional tradition has developed its own set of conventions and stylemes, as regards reading pace, drawing style, subject matter and themes. Each of these regional varieties of comics can thus be seen as a 'dialect' of the language of comics.
>
> (Zanettin, 2008: 18)

Zanettin goes on to suggest that the 'study of translated comics may provide useful insights into an understanding of translation as a complex process of intercultural communication, involving much more than simply the replacement of written text in speech balloons' (2005: 98). Thinking along similar lines, Altenberg and Owen write that 'the linguistic translation of comics has some distinct practical issues: spatial issues akin to those in subtitling, to do with fitting the new language into the extant text boxes and speech balloons' (2015: i). However, they suggest that it is in the translation of meaning that problems occur: 'Undertaking to translate that meaning can entail: rewriting text with no redrawing, rewriting text with partial redrawing, rewriting text with complete redrawing, or retaining the text with complete redrawing' (2015: i). There are many arguments that can be made for and against image translation, and these topics form the basis of much work being done in Comics and translation studies, by scholars including Zanettin, Altenberg, and Klaus Kaindl. Kaindl writes: 'If we do not translate languages but cultures, what is the role of the non-verbal dimension in translation: do we have to redefine the concept of translation in order to also include forms of transfer which do not involve language?' (2004: 174). It is difficult to deny that the translation of comics at the level of the image and sign is essential to the proper cross-cultural trans-mission and understanding of Comics. If, as Berman claims, 'a translator without historical consciousness is a crippled translator, a prisoner of his representation of translation and of those carried by the social discourses of the moment', it is not an exaggeration to say that, in Comics, a translator who does not consider the visual element is similarly hindered in their enterprise (Berman, qtd in Venuti, 2012: 2). We also need to remember that there is an economic element in this equation and that the widest possible distribution of a work is financially advantageous. There are those who seek to distribute translated works for other reasons, which will be discussed further in relation to *Manga* later in this chapter.

Cultural practices

Marta Breen and Jenny Jordahl's 2018 comic *Women in Battle* was originally published in Norwegian as *Kvinner I Kamp,* and it has since been translated into twelve languages. Breen and Jordahl's comic consists of fourteen vignettes of key women in the history of feminism and the women's movement. Breen's gentle, witty writing and Jordahl's simple, clear-lined accompanying visual images work well together. This comic translates well into various languages, largely because the images contain few culturally specific codes and the textual components are clearly demarcated from the images making word-for-word translation comparatively straightforward. However, this is not to say that *Women in Battle* did not encounter problems generated by the demands of some of the target languages (and markets) into which it was translated. For example, there are two English language versions, with the titles *Women in Battle* (UK) and *Fearless Females* (US). The chapter about the history and development of contraception begins with the work of Margaret Sanger and ends with the sexual revolution of the 1960s and 1970s. The final image is a double-page bleed of a party in full swing. In the UK version, many of the female characters are drawn topless, with breasts exposed, as shown in Figure 3.1. In the US version, artist Jordahl was compelled by law to cover the topless women with t-shirts, in accordance with various regulations forbidding the displaying of women's nipples. This is an example of a redrawn image that does not involve making an alteration to the text. The US's federal legal structures

Figure 3.1 Women in Battle (p. 173) by Marta Breen and Jenny Jordahl (2018).

also demand that such laws normally fall under the jurisdiction of the member states individually, but even so, for print or online publication purposes, displaying women's nipples is prohibited.

The difference between the inclusion or removal of topless female images is indicative of a cross-cultural issue of translation that relates directly to a larger question of cultural practice. This points to the fact that translation can be *within* a language, as well as *across* languages. Many argue that British and American English are distinct dialects of an imaginary core 'English' along with other Englishes spoken in Australia, large parts of post-colonial Africa, India, and the Caribbean. These Englishes are, on the whole, mutual intelligible, and they share a number of common etymological roots. As Weissbort and Eysteinsson observe: 'There are, of course, many Englishes today, which are similar enough not yet to require by and large the work of translators to ensure their mutual intelligibility, even if the possibilities of misunderstanding are considerable' (2006: 5). It is easy for those of us in the Anglosphere to forget that there are many Englishes and that native speakers of English are able, on the whole, to move between them with ease, compared to speakers of other languages. However, the risk of misunderstanding and the need for culturally specific changes to non-linguistic aspects of the text remain. Though it is not necessary for translators to be involved *per se*, there is still a need for cross-cultural expertise in the movement of texts across national-cultural boundaries since, as Weissbort and Eysteinsson observe, cross-cultural communication involves translation (Weissbort and Eysteinsson, 2006: 5).

(American) Football versus soccer

Jokes are usually culturally and linguistically specific and are among the most difficult parts of any text to translate. However, in Comics, many of the jokes are visual and so demand a different kind of translation that, sometimes, is not effective. One such example appears in the long-running and internationally famous comic strip *Peanuts* (1950–2000, ending with the death of the creator Charles Schulz). One running gag (a common feature of comic strips) involves Charlie Brown and Lucy van Pelt. Lucy is holding an American football and, whenever Charlie Brown moves to kick it, she moves it out of his reach forcing him to fall to the ground, as shown in Figure 3.2. The joke is dependent on

Figure 3.2 Panels from *Peanuts* by Charles Schulz (1950–2000).

an understanding of a culturally specific sport: American football. Holding the ball, as Lucy does, is necessary for the player to make the kick in American football. This makes perfect sense to an American reader, and this knowledge is crucial for the joke to work correctly. However, the same image translated into German does not work, as Kaindl explains

> [In] the German version, as published in the magazine *Stern*, the oval American football is replaced by the round (soccer) ball more commonly found in Europe [...] In the German version with a round ball used for soccer, whose rules do not permit players to touch the ball, the act of holding the ball appears unmotivated or to serve no other purpose than pulling it away, thus rendering the gag much less effective.
>
> (Kaindl, 2004: 184)

The comic effect of the joke is lost because it is dependent on sporting regulations that do not translate into the codes of other cultures.

Name puns across languages

In a large range of humour comics, many of the jokes come from names and name puns. This is especially true of René Goscinny and   Albert Uderzo's long-running *Astérix* series (first published in French in 1959, with English translations appearing in 1969). The series follows life in a small Gaulish village during the time of the Roman Empire whose occupants are holding out against their Roman conquerors, thanks in part to a magic potion brewed by the village druid. The villagers range from a fishmonger and mechanic to the village bard and a spritely 90-year-old. All Gaulish characters have names that end in '-ix', which adapt the Roman form of names originally given to Gaulish leaders such as Vercingetorix (82 B CE–46 BCE) and Dumnorix (first century BCE, dates unknown). The names of all characters refer to their roles in the village or to some aspect of their personality through adapting aspects of the French language to appear in mock-Romanised form. These names are linguistically specific, but they combine Latin and French, and they therefore require careful translation as the series moves between languages.

Let us take as an example the character of the Gaulish village chief, a short, fat man with pigtails, often seen being carried on a shield. In the original French version of the series, he is called 'Abraracourcix'. The name is from *à bras raccourcis* (with shortened arms) which comes from the phrase *tomber sur quelqu'un à bras raccourcis* (to attack someone with violence). This linguistic pun does not work in other languages such as in the British English version where he becomes 'Vitalstatistix' (from 'vital statistics', the basic information contained in population records) or in American English where he is 'Macroeconomix', a pun on his leadership role's bureaucratic potential; the German translation maintains the leadership focus but removes the bureaucratic slant, calling him 'Majestix'. In the Serbian translation the character is Дрматорикс (Drmatoriks), a pun on *drmator*, a slang term similar to 'mover and shaker', taken from the verb *drmati* (to shake). The word is often associated with Serbian Communism and carries a cultural weight that is not easily translated into a single equivalent word in other languages. Thus, in order for the joke to work, each name needs to be translated, not only into the target language but also in a way that makes sense to both the target language group and that reflects the meaning inherent in the source text.

National-cultural comics traditions

Bandes Dessinées

It may seem curious that comics from France and Belgium are often grouped together. This is less a question related to national origin than to the language that unites them, and it may therefore be more logical to refer to *Bandes Dessinées* (literally 'strip drawings'; often rendered *BDs*) as Francophone comics. France and a large proportion of Belgium, as well as Switzerland, Luxembourg, and Monaco all share the same language, and this helps to create a market that erodes national boundaries. Many *Bandes Dessinées* are widely read outside of Europe in other

Francophone territories such as Québec, and parts of Africa, the Middle East, and Asia that were previously under French or Belgian colonial rule. It is important to note that the title *Bandes Dessinées* does not carry the same stigma as Comics, and Francophone scholarship regularly refers to the form as *le neuvième art* (the ninth art), a term coined by film critic Claude Beylie in 1964.

In contrast to the Anglophone markets in the US and UK, *BDs* were available in bound books much earlier in their publication histories. Since 1945, the majority of works have been published as 'albums', hardback, full-cover books that are roughly A4 size. Each album (also called '*tomes*' in French) usually contains a complete narrative arc, similar to the modern graphic novel rather than to most newsstand comic books of the 1940s and 1950s.In earlier times, they consisted of stories that had been previously serialised in magazines or supplements that would then be collected. Since the 1980s, this has ceased to be the case since a number of writers and stories now appear *only* in album form. Each album typically has 46 or 62 pages, plus 2 end pages, a factor that is largely due to a standard printing convention, which favours multiples of 8. Modern print technologies are now making such standards redundant but they do remain for some publishers (see Grove, 2010; Miller, 2007).

The history of *BDs* follows a similar path to Anglophone Comics in that they also have developed out of political cartooning and text-image stories, such as the works of Rodolphe Töpffer (see Chapter 2), before moving into newspapers and magazine supplements. *Bécassine*, a short strip by Jacqueline Rivière and Joseph Pinchon about a Breton girl of the same name, appeared in *La Semaine de Suzette* on 2 February 1905, making her one of the first women of *BDs*. Another early strip, *Les Pieds Nickelés* by Louis Forton, premiered on 4 June 1908 in the newspaper *L'Épatant* (Lehembre, 2005). Both *Bécassine* and *Les Pieds Nickelés* were drawn in 'text comic' style, with the image and text caption separated, as was typical of *BDs* at the time. It was only with the 1925 launch of Alain Saint-Ogan's *Zig et Puce* that the 'text comic' style was replaced with speech bubbles and fully integrated text, a feature that we now think of as the recognisable modern Comics style. Matthew Screech suggests that Saint-Ogan's comic is the moment where 'all of the requirements for a modern *BD* came together for the first time' (2005: 6).

Although there are other contenders for the position, the first modern *BD* is probably Hergé's *Les Aventures de Tintin* (*The Adventures of Tintin*). The initial story arc, *Tintin in the Land of the Soviets,* was first published in *Le Petit Vingtième,* a children's supplement to the newspaper *Le Vingtième Siècle,* in 1929. *Tintin* was an immediate success, and the stories were published in album format immediately following their run in the newspaper. This makes Hergé's work the first modern *BD* to be published in album form, and *Tintin in the Land of the Soviets* was the first to appear as an individual book in 1930. However, despite its enduring popularity, *Tintin* is not without controversy. Some stories include racist or political stereotyping that does not easily translate into the contemporary world. One much-discussed example is *Tintin in the Congo* (1931), in which Tintin travels to the Congo which was still a Belgian colony at that time. Hergé depicted the Congolese as 'good at heart but backwards and lazy, in need of European mastery' (McCarthy, 2006: 37). Hergé's racist depictions are clear, but his intentions are not, with scholars divided on the issue of whether he was 'more patronising than malevolent' (Thompson, 1991: 43), or that 'when it was fashionable to be a colonial racist, that's what he was' (Grove, qtd in Smith, 2010: n.p.). Scholars are also critical of the amount of animal cruelty in the story, with the representation of acts involving the blowing up of a rhino and poaching (see Met, 1996).

The Adventures of Tintin is rightly considered one of the most important *BDs* that inspired many later artists and writers. Having observed how successful the Tintin stories were in *Le Petit Vingtième,* other magazines followed suit. In 1938, Rob-Vel created Spirou, a bellboy and the titular character of *Spirou* magazine for Dupuis, one of the most successful *BDs* publishing houses still operating. American imports were popular at the time, but the Second World War made importing American comics increasingly difficult. Some Francophone artists used the opportunity to continue stories from American superhero comics while others, such as André Franquin, Peyo, and Albert Uderzo, found a market for their original creations, launching them on long and illustrious careers. This is not to say that American comics did not find a healthy readership when their post-war importation became possible. Nor does it deny that American themes were not popular with French-speaking audiences. It is no coincidence that Morris' cowboy series *Lucky Luke* (launched in 1946) has much in common with American Western comics. But there is a distinct artistic style, brand of humour, and publication structure that governs *BDs* in ways that are not typical in other countries. One of the most recognisable aspects is the artistic style known as *Ligne Claire*. The term comes from Dutch artist Joost Swarte (originally rendered *Klare Lijn*), first used in 1977 (Miller, 2007: 18). The style 'privileges smooth, continuous linework, simplified contours and bright, solid colours, while avoiding frayed lines, exploded forms and expressionistic rendering' (Hatfield, 2005: 60). *Ligne Claire* is more than just an artistic style: it carries tremendous iconic weight, thanks to its associations with certain artists and publications. Bruno Lecigne argues that 'the ideological efficacy of the *Ligne Claire* lies not in what is chosen for depiction, but in the idea that the world is legible' (Lecigne, qtd in Miller, 2007: 19). This manner of representation remains in common usage in *BDs*, thereby consolidating its place as an iconic referent to *BD* in general.

As we saw in Chapter 2, moral panics surrounding the reading of popular, low forms led to legislation to control youth engagement with comics in the UK and the US in the 1950s. Similar concerns were voiced in France and Belgium, although Francophone artists also wanted to protect their own work by trying to prevent American material to enter the market. As Miller puts it, in France this led 'the Communist Party to form a temporary alliance with Catholic pressure groups in order to draft a law aiming at the "protection" of young people' (Miller, 2007: 19). The *Loi du 16 Juillet 1949 sur les publications destinées à la jeunesse* (Law of 16 July 1949 on publications intended for young people) prohibited

[t]he publication of material destined for young people which presents immoral or criminal behaviour in a positive light, or which might otherwise demoralize young people. It also prohibits the display of violent or licentious material, whether or not it is intended for young people, in places where minors might be exposed to it, thereby allowing for censorship to be exercised over adult publications.

(Miller, 2007: 19)

As with the CCA regulations in North America, which came five years later, this law was intended for the protection of young readers. It effectively banned American comics, while at the same time protecting Francophone artists. However, it also had an unintended effect of hampering creativity, despite the fact that the influential *Pilote* magazine, which featured René Goscinny and Albert Uderzo's *Astérix* as the central series, had appeared in 1959, almost a decade earlier than the public protests of May 1968, which led to fundamental changes in the social and political structures of France.

Pilote was aimed at teenagers and students and it was very popular: the first issue sold 300,000 copies (Miller, 2007: 21). It retained its popularity after the events of May 1968, though the protests were central to the counter-culture movement and the development of new, underground publications. The American underground comix movement was influential in Europe, but many of the new Francophone magazines were widely and openly available, unlike their North American counterparts. For example, *Métal Hurlant* (1974–1987) was a science fiction and fantasy magazine, a vehicle for the exquisite artwork of Mœbius and Druillet's 'visionary mysticism' (Miller, 2007: 26). As Miller writes, 'in the work of Druillet, science fiction was not mere escapism but took on a metaphysical dimension, influenced by [horror writer H.P.] Lovecraft' (2007: 26). *Métal Hurlant*, like its Anglophone cousin *2000 AD*, became a key text for 1970s and 1980s nerd culture, whose influence is still recognised in both Comics and Science Fiction.

As in the case of the Anglophone graphic novel that became more common, eventually cementing its place in popular culture, the Francophone graphic novel pursued a similar trajectory. The Belgian magazine *(À Suivre)*, first published in 1977, popularised *Roman BD* (novel *BD*) as a term for self-contained, often more mature, narratives. In the 1990s, the *BD* received a further impetus with its expansion of publication opportunities as a large number of independent publishers sought to cash in on its success. The most influential is L'Association, established in 1990 by a small group that included artists Lewis Trondheim and David B. The growth and general acceptance of independent publishing led to a restructuring of both the production and marketing of *BDs,* providing opportunities for previously underrepresented artists and characters. The contemporary *BD*, like its international cousins, has become a diverse, nuanced, and culturally specific form that has developed from a rich and complex tradition of visual storytelling. A wide selection of *BDs* has been translated or adapted into other languages, and the form continues to be an important component of Francophone artistic and narrative identity.

Manga

As with other histories of Comics, it is impossible to precisely determine the birth of *Manga*. Its history is hotly debated by historians of Japan and Japanese culture, with writers divided into roughly two camps. On one side, scholars such as Adam Kern and Kinko Ito suggest that *Manga* in the modern sense is a continuation of Japanese visual–cultural traditions that date back to the *Edo* (1603–1867) and *Meiji* (1868–1912) periods or earlier. What we think of as *Proto-Manga* dates back to twelfth–century painted scrolls, especially *Chōjū-jinbutsu-giga* (literally 'animal–person caricatures'), many of which contain some sort of narrative, albeit without many of the expected features of modern *Manga*; their relationship is similar to that of the modern Western comic and the works of Hogarth, for example (see Chapter 2). The other side of the argument suggests that *Manga* became a recognisable form in Japan only during the Allied occupation (1945–1952) and that the cultural imports of the US during this period were the most important influences on the growth of what has become the modern *Manga* form. Although there are compelling arguments on both sides, it is difficult to dismiss the large numbers of early *Manga* that date from before 1945 and that display clear evidence of the residual influence form as it developed as far back as the *Edo* period. Japanese journalist Kanta Ishida discusses the work of Isao Takahata, who is most well-known as the founder of *anime* production company *Studio Ghibli*. Ishida suggests that 'there is no connection between *Chōjū-jinbutsu-giga* and contemporary Manga'; he accuses scholars of not treating the scrolls as masterpieces in their own right and says they are 'cubby-holed as just the origin of Manga' (Ishida, qtd in Loo, 2008: n.p).

It may be unfair to treat these historical examples simply as part of a myth of origins, yet seeing them as part of the wider history of *Manga* should not diminish their importance in the evolution of the form. Ito observes that:

> Like any other form of visual art, literature, or entertainment, *Manga* does not exist in a vacuum. It is immersed in a particular social environment that includes history, language, culture, politics, economy, family, religion, sex and gender, education, deviance and crime, and demography. *Manga* thus reflects the reality of Japanese society, along with the myths, beliefs, rituals, tradition, fantasies, and Japanese way of life.
>
> (2005: 456)

Chōjū-jinbutsu-giga is often cited as a precursor to *Toba-e*, printed image in accordion-style books following the style of Bishop Toba (Kern, 2006: 61). Often, the stories were localised and designed to appeal to fans of a local celebrity or *Kabuki* actor, but they clearly anticipate the style of *Manga* and should be labelled *proto-Manga*. But regardless of whether or not we accept the earliest scrolls as being a part of that history, there *are* clear proto-comics that appeared in the late eighteenth and early nineteenth centuries, including links to *Kamishibai*, a form of street performance (see Nash 2009), and *Kibyoshi*, picture books from the eighteenth century (see Kern 2006). The term *Manga* was popularised with the publication of the *Hokusai Manga* (published 1814–1878).

The *Hokusai Manga* is not a *Manga* in the modern sense of the word. Katsushika Hokusai is perhaps more famous, in the West, at least, for his woodblock print 'The Great Wave off Kanagawa' (c. 1833). His *Manga* comprises a collection of sketches and drawings akin to an archive of reference material. It contains no discernible narrative, though some pages can be read as very short narratives of movement (as in Figure 3.3, which shows a visual guide to self-defence techniques). It is Hokusai who is credited with coining the word *Manga*, though he is not the inventor of the form itself (Koyama-Richard, 2007: 64). He is, however, to be credited with increasing its popularity and reach.

The impetus for the entry of *Manga* into the mainstream in Japan is very similar to that which took place in the West: its appearance in newspapers. Anglophone expatriates in Japan had imported illustrated magazines, such as *Punch*, and comic strip

Figure 3.3 Image from *The Hokusai Manga* by Katsushika Hokusai (1760–1849) CC BY-SA 3.0.

supplements began to appear in Japanese newspapers by the end of the 1890s. In 1900, the *Jiji Shinpō* newspaper that launched the *Jiji Manga* was also the newspaper that printed the first modern Japanese comic strip, by Rakuten Kitazawa, beginning in 1902 (Gravett, 2004: 21). The popularity of *Manga* increased, and by the 1930s, monthly magazines that collected comic strips for both girls and boys were selling in large numbers (see Schodt, 1996). The growth in both popularity and diversity of *Manga* available was hampered by the Second World War and the Allied occupation of Japan. Although the occupation put in place a strict set of censorship policies, these did not cover *Manga,* and the postwar period saw a blossoming in creativity that led to the launch of two of the most successful *Manga* series of all time: *Sazae-san* (which literally means 'Ms Sazae', created in 1946 by Machiko Hasegawa) and *Mighty Atom* (*Astro Boy* in English translation, created in 1951 by Osamu Tezuka).

Sazae-san and Mighty Atom may appear to be very different characters and, in many ways, they are. Sazae-san is a strong female character, described by psychoanalyst Hayao Kawai as a 'woman of endurance' (1996: 125). She stands against the feminine ideal which had been ingrained in many by the Japanese imperial military regime, and the character subverted many cultural taboos. Mighty Atom, in contrast, is a naïve little boy (and super powered android) who, after being abandoned by his creator, is adopted by Professor Ochanomizu, and the pair then goes on adventures together. Despite their differences, *Sazae-san* and *Mighty Atom* are both narratives about family and the importance of affiliation in mid-twentieth century Japan, and both exerted an undeniable impact on the future of *Manga*. Since their first creations in the late 1940s and 1950s, they have sold 62 million and 100 million copies respectively. It is important to note that, like Anglophone comics of the period, *Manga* in the 1950s and 1960s appealed to all ages and genders, and the two most popular and profitable market genres of *Manga* are *Shōjo* (aimed at girls) and *Shōnen* (aimed at boys).

Since 1969, with the *début* of the 'Year 24 Group', a group of female artists who were all born around 1949, *Shōjo* has been drawn primarily by women artists. The group included award-winning artists such as Hagio Moto who was also known as 'the founding mother of modern *Shōjo*', Riyoko Ikeda, and Ryoko Yamagishi (Thorn, 2001: n.p). This new group of creators often told stories of strong, independent women who defied Neo-Confucianist gender roles (Yoshizumi, 1995). One such *Manga* is Riyoko Ikeda's 1971 *Berusaiyu no Bara* (The Rose of Versailles), in which a cross-dressing woman leads Marie Antoinette's personal guard. *Shōjo* focuses not only on the experiences of female characters, but also on their emotions and feelings. In order to represent these emotional lives effectively, this *Manga* employs borderless panels and complex, beautifully designed images, referring to them as 'picture poems' (1986: 88). There are many subgenres within *Shōjo*, including romance (*Redisu*), superheroines (*Redikomi*) and 'Ladies Comics' (*Josei*), and many of them overlap (Ōgi, 2004: 782).

Modern *Shōjo* is often concerned with love and romance, and these themes are usually paired with narratives of personal growth and 'coming of age'. According to Eri Izawa, 'the Japanese are romantic – imaginative, sentimental, individualistic, passionate' and romance 'symbolizes the emotional, the grand, the epic: the taste of heroism, fantastic adventure, and the melancholy; passionate love, personal struggle, and eternal longing' (2000: 138). Many of these qualities are found in *Yaoi* (also known as boys' love), a subgenre of *Shōjo* that features sexual relationships between male characters (typically teenagers), written by and for women. *Yaoi* developed from fan and *dōjinshi* cultures (see Chapter 4). It is a portmanteau of *yamanashi ochinashi iminashi* (no climax, no point, no meaning) and was first used in the 1970s. Enthusiasts would redraw their favourite characters in sexually explicit situations as a type of reader engagement.

Manga aimed at male readers is as diverse as that for female readers, with variants including *Shōnen* (for boys) and *Seinen* (for young men). *Shōnen* in the 1950s centred on science fiction and adventure stories, but superheroes were not popular. While war comics flourished in the Anglosphere, especially those that focussed on the Second World War, this theme did not translate easily into *Manga* because they could be seen as glorifying Imperial Japan. That said, fantasy and historical adventure stories were, and remain, very popular, as are those that feature martial arts, quests, and the supernatural. *Shōnen* and *Seinen* account for the majority of the most successful *Manga* series, as rated by sales numbers. The most successful to date is *One Piece* by Eiichiro Oda (1997–present), which has sold 462 million copies to date. The series follows Monkey Luffy, a young man who wants to be a pirate and so assembles his own crew of monsters and colourful characters. A number of other popular series are tied to *anime* (animated television) series: examples include *Naruto* (1999–2014), *Dragon Ball* (1984–1995), and *Attack on Titan* (2009–present). The impact of these comic magazines on Japanese culture generally cannot be underestimated; as Kinko Ito writes:

> A total of 278 comic magazines were published in 1998, for example, and the estimated number of copies published was 1,472,780,000 (Ito, 'The World'). Manga is read by all people in Japan, ubiquitous in a society that boasts one of the highest literacy rates in the world. *Manga* affects behaviour and social trends by creating booms in sports and hobbies in Japan. Some criminals testified in court that they got their ideas from *Manga*.
>
> (2005: 473)

The use of *Manga* as a means for providing new models of criminal enterprise may be empirically questionable, but Ito is clear that the form itself is central both to Japanese cultural engagement and to national identity, a statement that does not hold for most Anglophone traditions. The cross-fertilisation of other traditions with *Manga* has led to a number of what we may call 'fusion' publications, such as *La Nouvelle Manga* or the *Franga* movement in France, *Spaghetti Manga* in Italy and 'Amerimanga' in the US (Zanettin, 2008: 5).

Manga are published in a range of formats. Typically, a series will begin in an anthology magazine alongside other series. These magazines are colloquially known as 'phone books' and contain between 200 and 800 pages. When a series has proved successful, it will be printed as *Tankōbon*, roughly equivalent to a graphic novel. Internationally, many *Manga* are available as 'scanlation', a portmanteau of 'scan' and 'translation' that refers to 'the practice of domesticating *Manga* for free digital distribution without the legal right to do so' (Brienza, 2016: n.p.). In her study of *Manga* as an international phenomenon, Casey Brienza explains that,

> [D]ue to their particular skill set, many people now working in the industry [...] were themselves former scanlators. In spite of that, from the publishing industry's perspective, scanlations are blatant digital piracy, and since the economic downturn of 2008, views on scanlations have hardened considerably.
>
> (2016: n.p.)

Scanlations circulate on the internet, on image-based websites, or are accessible as downloadable files. The history of scanlation distribution began with the translation of *Manga* scripts, and although separate from the *Manga* itself, the two would be read alongside each other. Early scanlations were distributed among enthusiasts through postal mail, and with the rise of the internet and free websites (such as Geocities), scanlations moved online. In the twenty-first century, most scanlations are 'distributed to readers through platforms such as IRC, and BitTorrent and various sites index and aggregate large numbers of scanlated works' (Brienza, 2016: n.p.). This is a collaborative activity, with large groups of individuals working on each text, often communicating with other groups or belonging to several groups simultaneously. Each group will organise its own labour structures, and the leadership or management structures may be unique to each group.

In ethical terms, scanlation is problematic in that, strictly speaking, it involves copyright violation and is therefore illegal. Even so, there are many good arguments for the original authors for permitting it. Douglass, Huber, and Manovich claim that high levels of interest and enthusiasm, paired with slow and drawn out delays with official translation, is the reason for the creation and rapid growth of scanlation groups. Many scanlators and scholars of the form highlight the altruistic and community nature of the groups, although Donovan has suggested that the primary objective of all scanlators is simply self-promotion (2010: 13). In 2010, a legal action was taken against scanlation and Calvin Reid has observed that

> Many manga publishers and retailers who used to believe that scanlations actually attracted new readers, now blame the sales decline on the rise of giant for-profit scanlation sites that have allowed a new generation of fans to grow up reading manga for free online.
>
> (Reid, 2010: n.p.)

It is true that the practice and sharing of scanlation did allow a wider readership of *Manga* to develop, especially in countries and languages where official translations were not available, or where communities of enthusiasts were very small. Nor, according to Reid, did translation into other languages result in the decline of scanlation versions of Manga as had originally been thought (Reid, 2010). Without the kind of sharing involved in scanlation, one might argue that international interest in *Manga* may not have developed to anywhere near the extent that it has. However, this does not obscure the fact that scanlation remains technically illegal. Even so, while scanlation is still available freely online, the responsibility rests with the readers to decide for themselves whether they wish to access these sites.

Smaller national comics traditions

Manga circulate widely and are now, along with their offshoots, a truly global form, but there also exist a number of much smaller, national comics forms. For example, Italian-language comics called 'Fumetti', which literally means 'little smoke puffs', a reference to speech bubbles, are a rich and thriving industry, containing both translations and original language material. The first Italian comics appeared on newsstands in 1908, with the launch of *Il Corriere dei Piccoli* (Courier of the Little Ones), a comics magazine aimed at children. The magazine featured a mixture of original material and translated reprints. One original character is *Bilbolbul*, created by Attilio Mussino, a little boy who was perhaps the first Italian Comics character. In addition, many American strips were imported into Italy and 'Italianised': for example, *The Katzenjammer Kids* became *Bibì e Bibò,* and *Felix the Cat* became *Mio Mao.*

As with many other European countries, the Second World War caused a marked shift in the availability of imported material and the way that Comics was used locally. The Italian fascist regime had already harnessed the potential of the form for propaganda through the creation of 'educational' comics for young people, notably *Il Giornale dei Balilla* (1923) and *La Piccola Italiana* (1927). The prohibition of foreign comics between 1939 and 1945 resulted in some publishers simply changing the names of characters to disguise their origins, while some developed their own versions of a known character, as is the case of *Topolino* (Mickey Mouse's Italian double), published in Italy until 1988.

Since the late 1940s, the majority of comics in Italy have been printed in 'Bonelliano' format, a term named after the publisher that developed the style. These are bound books containing one complete story of over 100 pages, drawn in black-and-white artwork. In the 1970s and 1980s, the underground comics movement centred in Bologna. Italian artists were heavily influenced by the American comix movement and, as with other countercultural comix movements, this gave them the freedom to experiment with artistic styles and themes. Of those Italian comics read internationally, one of the most famous is *Corto Maltese* (1967–1989), created by Hugo Pratt. Maltese is a dashing sea captain, living in the early twentieth century, whose adventures cover a large geographic area and include meetings with historical figures like the Western outlaw Butch Cassidy and the First World War German flying ace the Red Baron. Simone Castaldi writes that the move from newsstand to bookshop has led to 'a few new bestselling authors such as Gipi, Francesca Ghermandi, and Zerocalcare, […] providing a chance for national revitalisation of the form' (2017: 83).

Comics in Spain emerged in the late nineteenth century, with popular satirical magazines, like *La Flaca* (1869–1876) or *El Mundo Cómico* (1873). The most influential comic in the history of Hispanic comics is *TBO*, a magazine published from 1917 to 1998. *TBO* published both local and imported strips, mostly aimed at children, and many of them featured slapstick humour. Castaldi notes that

> [T]he magazine's name has become so synonymous with the form that to this day, comics are referred to in Spain as either '*Historietas*' or '*Tebeos*' – the latter a play on the acronym *TBO*, which sounds like the Spanish '*te veo*' or 'I see you'.
>
> (2017: 83)

As with the Mussolini dictatorship in pre-war Italy, censorship during the Franco regime in Spain was very strict. Superhero stories were prohibited, and local comics used historical figures instead. Medieval heroes were especially popular, such as *El Guerrero del Antifaz* (*The Masked Warrior*) created by Manuel Gago in 1944 and *Capitán Trueno*, created by Víctor Mora and Miguel Ambrosio Zaragoza in 1956. Many scholars consider this to be a high point in the history of Spanish Comics (see Porcel, 2002; Merino, 2003). A distinctive style emerged, which took its inspiration from Franco-Belgian authors such as Franquin, published by Editorial Bruguera. The most popular comic at the time was *Mortadelo y Filemón*, created in 1958 by Francisco Ibáñez Talavera. The main characters were stupid, mismatched private investigators, later secret agents, who routinely fail at every assignment in a slapstick and overtly cartoonish manner.

Censorship restrictions continued to tighten through the 1960s and the Spanish local industry has not been buoyant since magazines began to close in the 1970s. However, there have been some attempts to regenerate local industry to support Hispanophone creators. Since 1989, Barcelona has hosted an annual Comics convention and, in 2007, the Spanish Ministry of Culture launched *El Premio Nacional del Cómic* (National Comic Award) to support Spanish creators and thus reinvigorated the local industry.

Internationally, comics industries did not always follow similar growth trajectories, appearing first on newsstands and in satirical publications as they had done according to Western histories. The reasons for this are many, but they generally hinge

on localised attitudes towards Comics literacy rates and availability of publication outlets. This is not to say that comics were
not conspicuous outside Europe and North America; rather, the
ways in which they came into existence does not always follow
the dominant model discussed. It is true that, as we have already
seen, the history of forms like *Manga* followed a pattern similar
to that which prevailed in the West, but this is not necessarily
typical. Indeed, many emerging economies have developed and
are developing their own Comics industries and their own distinctive model of publication, and their histories are markedly
different from the model described earlier in Chapter 2 and elsewhere in this chapter.

India provides an excellent example of just such an emerging model. The local Indian market was not established until
1964, with the launch of *Indrajal Comics*, a magazine published
by the English-language newspaper *The Times of India*. Even so,
the magazine did not include original material, but reprints of
The Phantom (by Lee Falk, originally published in the US in the
1930s) and *Flash Gordon* with some aspects made more suitable
for a local audience. Because *Indrajal Comics* was published in
English, the majority of the population was not able to access it,
following the language barrier (approximately only 12% of the
population spoke English). Translations of American strips began
to appear in the late 1950s, and were very popular, especially
with younger readers.

In the 1960s, comics that were both written and produced
in India for a primarily Indian market started to be published.
The first Indian superhero, Batul the Great, began publication in 1962 in the magazine *Shuktara*. The character Batul was
successful, influenced both by a famous Bengali bodybuilder and
also Desperate Dan (from the Scottish publication *The Dandy*).
He was a muscular, all-powerful figure who could lift anything,
and he was indestructible. The most famous Indian comics of the
period was *Amar Chitra Katha* (ACK, literally 'immortal picture
stories'), created by Anant Pai in 1967. A potentially apocryphal
story about the company's founding states that Pai wanted to
help Indian children connect with their heritage after learning

that many students were well-versed in Greek and Roman myth-ologies but unaware of Indian mythologies and folklore (Babb and Wadley, 1998: 76–86). Pai's aim was threefold: to give Indian children a sense of their own heritage, to counter traditional colonial teaching that privileged Greek and Roman history, and to introduce students to the narratives of Indian history and mythology. Since the late 1960s, ACK has become one of the most successful publishers of comics in India, with adaptations of Indian mythological narratives, folklore, and religious texts, all aimed at young readers. The artwork is reminiscent of devotional images of Hindu deities, making it instantly recognisable and conferring a level of respectability and seriousness upon it that will guarantee its respectability. By the 1970s, Indian publishers began to create local versions of American superheroes, and that market remained relatively buoyant until the late 1990s, when it was overtaken by the rise of video games and the internet. Jeremy Stoll writes that 'with the arrival of liberalisation in 1991, the Indian economy was integrated into the global one, resulting in an overall shift to consumerism and greater international com-petition. Simultaneously, readers and creators had greater access to foreign media' (2017: 92).

Since the year 2000, the Indian Comics community has shifted from national publications to regional and small-press publications, but a number of creators has become internation-ally successful with their graphic novels. Amruta Patil's *Kari*, published in 2008, is a landmark text that demonstrates not only skilful use of the form but also contains innovation of storytelling and LGBT+ characters, previously relatively unrepresented in Indian comics. Other texts, such as *This Side, That Side* (edited by Vishwajyoti Ghosh and published in 2013), reframe complex and traumatic periods of Indian history, such as the 1947 division of the former British Indian Empire into the Union of India and the Dominion of Pakistan (commonly known as 'Partition'), in an accessible, effective, and rejuvenated form. In addition to being a popular market for graphic novels, India welcomed web comics, largely due to their ease of creation and dissemination. They are easily spread through social media, and many artists use them to educate younger readers on socially and politically charged topics such as feminism, domestic abuse, and voter rights (see section on 'Web comics' in Chapter 1).

This chapter and the preceding one have both shown how the histories of Comics are intertwined with histories of printing, political comment, censorship, and literacy. Furthermore, the histories and traditions of different countries intersect through conflict, occupation, and colonialism. The final country I discuss in this chapter offers a clear demonstration of the intersection of all these issues: the Republic of Korea. Korean comics are called *Manhwa* (만화 or 漫畵), which bears a linguistic similarity to the Japanese name. Between 1910 and 1945, Korea was occupied by Japan, and many elements of Japanese popular culture were integrated into Korean society. Political cartooning and comics had been published during the 1900s but most of these publications had been censored or shut down completely by 1920 (Russell, 2012). The term *Manhwa* came into common usage in the 1920s, referring specifically to children's comics.

As with other countries, the Second World War affected the transmission of published material both internationally and within national borders. By 1948, the newly formed Republic of Korea began to establish new press outlets, and this created new opportunities for political cartooning and comics in general; the first Korean comic was started in 1948 by Kim Yong-Hwan but was quickly closed, because it infringed obscenity regulations (Kim and Choe, 2014). *Manhwa* has struggled to be seen as distinct from *Manga*, especially in Western markets, where it is often published alongside Japanese language publications. However, this close cultural tie between the two traditions may have been to the benefit of Korean artists, *Manhwabang*, who were not culturally isolated, as others may have been, in small artistic communities. Instead, the cultural and artistic exchange between Japan and Korea helped to build up the small market and provide opportunities for Korean artists beyond the readership of their home country.

4 Cultures and commodities

The thing itself

Comics as a material 'thing' has a history that is bound up in production, publication, audience, fandom, and readership in a way that is unique, and paying attention to this can completely change the way we engage with and understand the form. As I suggested briefly in Chapter 2, the production and publication processes for Comics are different from most other types of book. Text-based literature (what we may call 'traditional book publishing' or 'the bookseller model') is sold primarily through publishing houses which offer contracts to authors, buy the rights to publish a text, and pay the author in advances and royalties. In recent years, this traditional model has been modified since self-publishing has gradually increased in popularity. Many comics are self-published by individual creators and then sold at conventions or online. The dominant model in mainstream comics is called the 'direct market', which emerged in the 1970s and was largely defined by the fact that retailers could not return unsold stock. As outlets were buying 'direct' from the publishers, the comics arrived quicker and in better condition. However, retailers also had to judge how many copies they were likely to sell, and over-estimation could be very costly. This label, however, is no longer strictly accurate since there is now a single distributor, Diamond Comics Distributors, that dominates the market, although the model remains the same. Developments in e-book technologies and the rise of the internet have led to changes in web publishing and digital distribution methods for comics. One example is ComiXology, probably the biggest digital distribution platform, which launched in 2013. Since then, this platform claims they have logged 200 million downloads and currently hosts more than 100,000 individual comics, and in June 2018, they launched ComiXology Originals, which facilitated a variant of self-publishing. All these mean that comics libraries can be entirely digital.

The comic book is a media artefact unlike others, and what has grown up around it is a rich and diverse network of physical and virtual spaces, practices, and communities that regularly come together to create the wider culture of Comics. 'Geek culture', as it is now called, does not begin and end with the comic book shop, but it now extends to incorporate conventions and online communities of enthusiasts, as well as permitting production of artefacts generated by readers themselves that include artwork, fan fiction, and cosplay (where participants dress as their favourite characters), extending to engagements with the creation process itself. In addition, we need to remember that Comics culture often intersects with other narrative forms and fan activities, including film and television, gaming, and role-play. This chapter will outline some of the key issues in the culture of Comics as a wider phenomenon and will consider what all this means for both creator and consumer and how these issues relate to the study of Comics.

Fan/geek/nerd/dork/other?

It is important to define the concept of fandom and to understand the complex social structures and nuances of fan communities. What does it mean to refer to somebody as a fan? In his book *Understanding Fandom*, Mark Duffett traces the use of the word 'fan' back to the late seventeenth century, 'where it was a common abbreviation for "fanatic" (a religious zealot)' (2013: 5). He goes on to remind us that 'it is easy to make swift generalizations and say that prototypical forms of fandom therefore never existed in earlier times. That would, however, mistake the invention of the label for the beginning of the phenomenon' (2013: 5). There have been enthusiastic followers of celebrities, writers, actors, and even religious figures, for centuries. A fan is not, however, a person who is simply fond of something. Harrington and Bielby claim that 'being a fan requires not only participation in activities but the adoption of a particular identity that is shaped through subjective and affective experiences' (1995: 97). The adoption of a fan identity is one of the reasons that the modern usage of the word is accompanied by connotations that are specific and generally negative. In her article on fandom as pathology, Joli Jensen writes that 'the literature on fandom is haunted by images of deviance' and she describes two characterisations of fans: the obsessed loner and the member of a hysterical crowd (1992: 9, 13). It would be more accurate to think of these as stereotypes because, by and large, they do not represent fandom. Of course, there are those in all kinds of fan communities whose interests border on obsession and there are also situations where large groups of fans, mainly young women, who may become 'hysterical'. However, this term is often used to describe any crowd. I will return to the issue of gender bias in fandoms later in this chapter. Generally speaking, fandom has been defined by some as 'a form of psychological compensation, an attempt to make up for all that modern life lacks' (Jensen, 1992: 16). Such definitions of this kind are both insulting and patently incorrect. Fan communities include a range of genders who engage in various kinds of production and consumption, who offer mutual support to their members, and who, most importantly, seek to enjoy themselves.

Of course, not all fandoms are created equal. We do not talk of the 'Opera Fandom' or the 'High Modernist Literature Fandom'. It is perfectly acceptable to be enthusiastically devoted to such things, and in possession of an encyclopaedic subject knowledge, but these are examples of the so-called 'high art', and we may be more likely to hear the term 'aficionado' than 'fan' applied to such enthusiasts. As Jensen points out, 'the obsession of a fan is deemed emotional (low class, uneducated), and therefore dangerous, while the obsession of the aficionado is rational (high class, educated) and therefore benign, even worthy' (1992: 21). It is the difference here between cultural approval and an activity that attracts a degree of stigmatisation. Paul Lopes quotes Goffman's seminal study of stigma, which argues that 'a stigmatized person's social identity is discredited by the power of a single attribute, such as being visually impaired or a drug user' (2006: 387). Lopes makes the point, however, that 'not all fandom is stigmatized […] It is the fandom of low-status popular culture that normals [a commonly used to term to distinguish fans and non-fans] view as problematic' (2006: 396). Moreover, fandom is often far more stigmatised than the artefact to which it is attracted: 'Trekkies are stigmatized, not the television show *Star Trek* and its offshoots' (Lopes, 2006: 396). According to 'the Geek Hierarchy', a sprawling, multi-directional flowchart created by Lore Sjöberg in 2002, there is always someone lower on the 'geek food chain'. However, much of this classification occurs within the community itself, and such hierarchies change when seen through the eyes of 'normals'.

Those who engage in 'low art' are classed very differently and 'the comic book becomes a sign of the asocial and obsessive individual, the geek or the dork' (Lopes, 2006: 407). It is amusing to observe the strange semantic contortions that some people go through to justify their interest in comics. One such example comes from a review of Marjane Satrapi's award-winning comics memoir *Persepolis* (2000) in *The Nation*. Here the reviewer begins by claiming defensively that, 'it has never been a habit of mine to read comics books,' but she then adds that she was surprised she enjoyed the book, and was even further surprised to find it to be so beautifully crafted (Wolk, 2007: 13). 'Serious' literary journalists, it would appear, do not regularly read comics and certainly not without carefully justifying themselves. Entry into the domain of Comics requires caution both because it is generally regarded as a low cultural form, but also because the kind of fandom it is perceived as attracting is both socially stigmatised and associated with deficient personality traits. Representative characterisations that appear in the parallel domain of popular film include the figure of Elijah Price in *Unbreakable* (2000), a comic book dealer and wheelchair user, who also perpetrates hideous acts of terrorism. Another example is comic book writer Holden McNeil in *Chasing Amy* (1997), whose actions are both predatory and homophobic. Such examples consistently portray comics fans negatively, and this contributes to a general perception of their common identity.

But who *are* these geeky, dorky, obsessive fans? What does a comics fan look like? When we conjure up a mental image of a 'comic book fan', the image that comes to mind is, perhaps, the obese, odious 'Comic Book Guy' from the long-running television show *The Simpsons* (1989–present) or the comics-devouring scientists of *The Big Bang Theory* (2007–2019). The 'typical fan' image may include certain clothing, levels of personal hygiene, tattoos, or body type, and it is likely that this imaginary person will be both white and male. Many of the fan characters we see in popular culture exhibit all these traits, along with social awkwardness and ineptitude in romantic matters; in fact, comics and the accompanying paraphernalia are often used as visual shorthand to denote these character traits. With this as the 'typical' image of a fan, both the issues of media representation and the stigma of fandom participation are clear. There is, however, a wider problem with this kind of representation. This image of fandom is largely applied to mainstream comics fans, as opposed to those who read mainly graphic novels or international publications, including *Manga*. But even then, 'typical' does not mean 'accurate' because most fans do not fit this stereotype. There are many levels of perception at play here, and the term 'geek' has become 'a common pejorative used within the subculture of comic books as a self-identification of fans as failures in the eyes of normals' (Lopes, 2006: 406). Clear and comprehensive statistics on comics readership are difficult to obtain for several reasons. As we have already seen, what constitutes a comic includes a variety of published forms, ranging from the bound book to the disposable magazine to digital content. Some people are regular readers, and some are occasional readers. The statistics that are available tend to focus on specific types or genres of comics, and they rely on either geographical determination, or on participants' self-identification. Figure 4.1 shows statistics on the purchases of over 70,000 people in the US that draw on information from book shops and comics-specific shops, in addition to internet purchases (Alverson, 2018: n.p.). What is immediately evident is that the

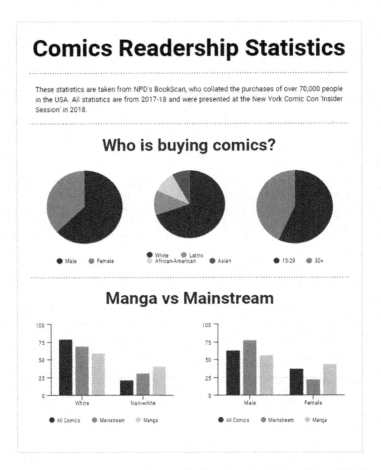

Figure 4.1 Statistics on comics readership, from NPD BookScan (2018).

majority of comics are bought by men, although the number is not substantial. Similarly, while most readers are white, there is solid representation from other ethnic groups. Most readers are young – under the age of thirty – but this statistic may be slightly skewed by the number of items purchased by individuals. For example, if a teenager buys five floppies (thirty-two-page, single-issue comics) for every single graphic novel bought by a forty-year-old, the statistics will be affected. When we examine the statistics in more detail by looking at specific genres of comics, we can notice the reader demographics change across both gender and race. When we compare *Manga* and mainstream sales, *Manga* is read (or at least purchased) by more women and people of colour than mainstream comics. This is the case with all comics, including graphic novels and international publications. The stereotypical image of the reader is not borne out by these statistics since readers of comics are as diverse as enthusiasts of any other narrative form. These statistics give a general overview of one of the largest book markets but are not complete since the focus is Anglocentric and does not consider the international consumer base (see Chapter 3).

Web comics pose a problem for statistics, as gathering methods rely on either web traffic, which does not take into consideration return visits, or self-identification, which some readers may resist. In addition, some individual web comics are hosted on several different websites, with no single 'publisher'. We do have statistics for one web comics portal, and this can provide a partial view. *WEBTOON* is the largest publisher of web comics in the world. In 2019, they reported viewing figures of 100 billion annually and over 15 million readers daily (Estlund, 2019). The platform hosts more than 1 million different titles from over 500,000 creators and is available both as a website and through a free mobile app. Each individual post includes a message board and options that allow for sharing across social media since a built-in community is an integral part of the platform. Perhaps most radically, in 2016 *WEBTOON* released a report which stated that 50% of their daily readers identified as female and 48% of comics uploaded featured female lead characters (MacDonald, 2016). There are several reasons for this apparent equality of gender representation. The most obvious reason is economic in that the access to content is free and includes the posting of new content on the site. As we will discuss in due course, the economic considerations of comics creation are of utmost importance to publishers, though this may not be fully reflected in the wishes or the enthusiasm of fans. As we saw in Chapter 1, web comics offer an opportunity for otherwise under-represented groups to create their own stories, and the statistics certainly bear this out. The freedom of the internet means that web comics (and digital comics) can tell stories that are not given space in the print realm.

Though some subforms of Comics, such as web comics, are making good strides in diverse representation, this is not the case in all areas. Before moving on to discuss the consumption spaces and different types of fan creation associated with Comics, we should pause to consider a controversy that has recently arisen within the American mainstream that has ramifications for fan engagement with the industry and fan interactions with each other in online spaces that affects the diversity of both artists and the representation of characters. The debate is known as 'Comicsgate' and has been described as a 'response to comic publishers', creators', and commentators' push for more representative titles [in which] white comics fans have harassed and boycotted said titles in the name of some kind of dated comics purity' (Passmore, 2019: 12). There had been rumblings within the mainstream fandom for some time as publishers introduced more female and minority ethnic characters. The 2016 release of *Mockingbird* by Chelsea Cain and Joëlle Jones became a focus of contention for many fans, as Cain wrote the female superhero in order to provide an explicit critique of many of the sexist and outdated aspects of the depiction of the superhero and accompanying tropes. The series was cancelled after eight issues, but the eighth featured a cover image of Mockingbird (Barbara 'Bobbi' Morse) in a t-shirt that read 'Ask me about my feminist agenda', and this image became emblematic of the main focus of dissatisfaction in Comicsgate.

However, in 2017 the debate resurfaced after a Twitter post by Marvel editor Heather Antos who posted a photograph of herself and other female Marvel colleagues enjoying a milkshake to celebrate their recently deceased colleague and long-standing Marvel employee Flo Steinberg (2017: n.p.). In response to this innocuous tweet, 'the women received scores of online abuse, calling them "fake geek girls", "social justice warriors", "virtue signallers", and they were accused of ruining the comics industry with their very presence' (Austin, 2019: 38). More worryingly, some of the women received rape or death threats or were 'doxxed' (a term used to describe the release of personal information online without the owner's consent). The campaign of abuse was headed by several male fans, using online resources including Twitter and 4chan to spread their message. The central thrust of their argument was that the original mainstream comics were not political at all and they claimed that these 'new hires' were making Comics too political. A brief glance at the cover of *Captain America #1*, in which Hitler is punched in the face, suggests that this claim is risible. Comics scholar Martin Lund suggests that this claim is indicative of 'the profound ignorance that the movement is based on' (2019: n.p.), and he goes on to suggest that the debate arose because of 'the general aversion to change that the genre is built upon and that is exacerbated by the demands to stick to formula that indefinite serial publication fosters' (n.p.).

This debate may appear to be little more than a group of hyper-committed fans refusing to adapt to the changes within the form as it engages with unavoidable cultural pressures. Their fan association with an existing community has been taken to the extreme in meeting change with hostility, demonstrating their reactionary claims of entitlement to, and ownership of, comics and characters (Austin, 2019). Hailey Austin describes the overt misogyny and racism that had prevailed of the Comicsgate debate: 'Women and minority groups can't be part of these communities because even thinking about them as participants breaks the image of the geek as solitary, disliked male' (39). Rather than positively embracing new readers for the industry, thereby promoting its continuation and ongoing development, these fans have taken an opposite view and regard the perceived failures of the industry as 'a direct result of hiring diverse talent and that [these people] need to be driven out' (Austin, 2019: 39). Their identity is threatened by what they perceive as an impending marginalisation, and they are reluctant to reconfigure their common identity in the light of the interests of new fans and new types of engagement.

The issues of Comicsgate extend beyond those who were directly confronted by campaigners. Very few Marvel employees spoke up in support of the artists and editors under attack but despite the critical acclaim that *Mockingbird* had accrued, it was cancelled in what might be regarded by some as a placation of the conservative bullying that became characteristic of Comicsgate. Proctor and Kies refer to such fan behaviour as 'toxic fan practices' (2018) which, they suggest, can take on a number of different forms, ranging from outright harassment including threats of violence or doxxing, to gatekeeping (blocking community entry to those not considered 'true fans') and the creation of a generally unpleasant environment. Comicsgate is the visible dimension of a deep-rooted campaign of misogyny, racism, and ableism (discrimination against people with disabilities) that pervades many fan cultures. This example is one that explicitly affects American mainstream Comics, one that has tightly controlled production practices and clearly defined fandoms. However, what is relevant to the American mainstream is not necessarily relevant to all areas of Comics. Still, it is one of the largest organisations within the domain of Comics and one that is internationally influential. Furthermore, Comicsgate is presented here as a case study of how fandom can create toxicity and lead to serious consequences for those involved in different aspects of industry, particularly at the level of the creation of pictorial representations, as well as to show how fan engagement can significantly affect industry decisions. This is, of course, not to suggest that all fan communities and cultures have this unsavoury discursive substructure that can exclude a large proportion of potential fans. It is, nonetheless, a phenomenon which can affect both the internal politics of a group and its public reception.

Consumption spaces

In what is now effectively the hyper-capitalist marketplace, comics are products that fans consume. Sandvoss writes, 'Given that fandom at its core remains a form of spectatorship, fan places are places of consumption' (2005: 53). Although 'spectatorship' is not always synonymous with 'consumption', in the case of purchasers of comics, their consumption includes not only both reading and interpreting the physical or electronic object, but also purchasing related media and merchandise. This activity is especially true of fans of mainstream comics, although the practice extends to popular sports and is a major source of income. In this section, we will focus on the communities that are constructed as sites of consumerism. In his book *Of Comics and Men: A Cultural History of American Comic Books*, Jean-Paul Gabilliet charts the rise (and fall) of comic book shops within the US (Gabilliet, 2010: 152). He notes a steady rise throughout the 1980s; less than 1,000 in 1981 growing to over 3,000 by 1985. These shops were responsible for 50% of all comics sales. Figures for 1992 show that the early 1990s were the peak for comics shops, with over 8,000 across the US, whereas by 2000, the number had dropped to 2,300. According to the statistics from *Publishers Weekly* in 2018, there were around 2,000 shops in the US (O'Leary, 2018: n.p.). Unlike many other specialist retailers, the comic book shop is not simply a place to purchase items, but an important gathering space for the community of fans. Matthew Pustz writes:

> The comic book shop is also a clubhouse, a place for discussion and debate. It is a kind of 'third place', somewhere that is neither home nor work but also somewhere one feels welcome and comfortable. Of course, fans have to establish their credentials to become part of the group […] Because of this, comic book shops have had the reputation of being exclusively for fans and not that friendly to outsiders who weren't able to establish their fan credentials.
>
> (2017: 271–272)

The clubhouse mentality that is so often found in comic shops creates a structure that reinforces a clear distinction between 'us' and 'them'. Those who 'speak the language' of the clubhouse and can prove their membership are accepted; those who do not, whose interests are not in line with the rest of the community, are made to feel alienated or uncomfortable. A long-running exaggerated stereotype of the comic shop in popular culture is that of a group of men standing to terrified attention like meerkats on the Serengeti as soon a woman walks in. There is much to suggest that these spaces are gendered, and according to Pustz, 'many women [are] turned off by posters celebrating acts of violence and often featuring supernaturally well-endowed, scantily clad female characters' (2017: 27). Despite such exclusivity and gatekeeping tactics, comic book shops remain a key feature of comics fan communities, although in recent years their numbers have dwindled because of the emergence of other comic genres and the shifts in consumer behaviour. Mark Rogers writes:

> This situation has changed somewhat in the twenty-first century. Driven by the popularity of *manga* and the increasing visibility of graphic novels in the American culture, comics publishing has moved strongly into the book distribution market. This exposes comics to a larger, more diverse audience and greater diversity in content has appropriately followed.
>
> (2012: 149)

In addition, other types of retail outlet, from bookshops to more generalised 'entertainment retailers', such as Forbidden Planet, are now large volume sellers of comics. This change in the locations of purchase can potentially change the cultural value of comics themselves; Gordon asks: 'Is there a greater degree of respectability attached to a book bought from a bookshop rather than a magazine from a newsstand or a comic book from a speciality store?' (2012: 161). There is no convincing answer to this question, but it does highlight the point that respectability in relation to the material object is often tied to the issue of location of purchase.

The other major site for fan consumption is the comic book convention (or 'con'), a place for fans to gather and interact with creators, publishers, and other fans. In addition to being spaces for the purchase of new comics and related fan paraphernalia, conventions usually also include panel discussions, lectures and workshops, debates, competitions, and information about new and upcoming releases and events. These gatherings borrow their format from science fiction conventions which came into existence in the 1930s and were originally run by fan-organised and not-for-profit organisations, though this is no longer the case for the majority of these events. There are conventions for every conceivable genre of comics, though the most famous of them concentrate their attention on the American mainstream. Figure 4.2 shows the breakdown of attendees at a range of fan events, by age, gender, and purpose of attendance. These statistics were gathered by Eventbrite, an online events management and

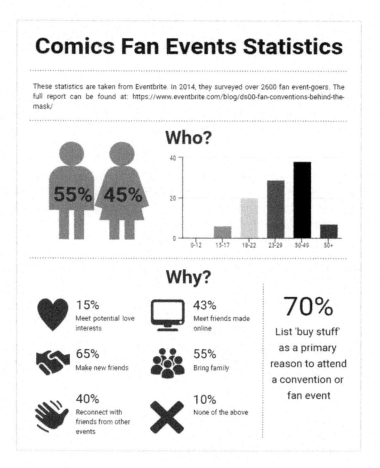

Comics Fan Events Statistics

These statistics are taken from Eventbrite. In 2014, they surveyed over 2600 fan event-goers. The full report can be found at: https://www.eventbrite.com/blog/ds00-fan-conventions-behind-the-mask/

Who?

55% 45%

Why?

15% Meet potential love interests

65% Make new friends

40% Reconnect with friends from other events

43% Meet friends made online

55% Bring family

10% None of the above

70% List 'buy stuff' as a primary reason to attend a convention or fan event

Figure 4.2 Statistics on comics fan event attendance, from Eventbrite (2014).

ticketing website. The data suggest that the events which form the basis of the research are smaller events, since larger gatherings tend to have their own ticketing infrastructure or use bigger management companies, including Ticketmaster. These statistics are useful, because they draw attention to the size and type of particular events. The breakdown shows a reasonably balanced gender split and a distribution of age that highlights issues such as age ranges, disposable income distribution, and details of the length of reading histories, all of which contribute to the construction and development of a fan identity. These statistics provide a good overview of the typical breakdown of comics cons, especially when we look at reasons for attendance at these conventions. Also, though they are places to register fan community and provide venues for socialising, the primary reason for their existence is as a marketplace for consumers. The most well-known convention is San Diego Comic-Con International (SDCC), held annually in San Diego since 1970. Despite the name, SDCC is no longer solely a comics convention since it now includes events such as discussion panels and launches for films and other related media, most of which is tied to the Marvel and DC cinematic industries. Despite its fame and appearance as a pop culture venue beyond the comics world, SDCC is no longer the largest convention of its type: that claim now is made by São Paulo's Comic Con Experience (founded in 2014). Even though it has lost its status, SDCC remains the most important event for American comics, as well as being the 'home' of the 'Will Eisner Comic Industry Awards', which have been presented at the convention since 1988. The Eisners, named after artist and writer Will Eisner, are awarded annually for achievement in American comic books and have thirty-one categories, including individual awards for all aspects of the creative process such as lettering, colouring, inking/pencilling, cover art, and writing.

Comics conventions are held all over the world and for all kinds of audiences. The Angoulême International Comics Festival (first held in 1974) is among the most prestigious for creators (and consumers) of *Bandes Dessinées*. The centrepiece of the festival is the announcement of award winners, with the 'main attraction' being the *Grand Prix*. With the full name of the *Grand Prix de la Ville d'Angoulême*, this award celebrates a lifetime achievement, but is awarded only to living creators, and never posthumously. The winner is made President of the next festival and hosts an exhibition of his or her own work. The *Grand Prix* became the source of some considerable controversy in 2016, when it became apparent that only one woman had ever won (Florence Cestac in 2000) and that that year's forty-name shortlist contained only cis men. This generated much discussion within the community, and many artists composed their responses in the form of short or single-panel comics. Figure 4.3 shows the response of Cestac. The female character on the left states that despite '43 festivals at *Angoulême,* only one woman has won the *Grand Prix*'; the male characters on the right affect mild surprise. Within Europe, the largest comic book convention is Lucca Comics & Games (first held in 1965), while the largest in Asia is *Comiket* (derived from Comic Market), held

Figure 4.3 Florence Cestac (2016). Courtesy of the artist.

twice yearly in Tokyo, boasting annual attendances of over half a million fans. Comiket is a fascinating example of a convention because, despite its now-massive size, it retains much of its original ethos as a grassroots, makeshift event focussed on the sale of *dōjinshi* (non-commercial, self-published *Manga*). It was founded in 1975 as a reaction to a *dōjinshi* creator being denied entry to a popular science fiction convention, and the first meeting had only 700 attendees. Although it is a not-for-profit, volunteer-run event, there is still some corporate presence from the biggest *Manga* publishers, but the majority of trading space is occupied primarily by amateur creators. Most trading participants do not make a profit, and as statistics from *Comiket* suggest, only 15% make money while another 15% break even. Attendance and engagement at *Comiket* are done very much for the love of the form rather than for commercial purposes.

One of the most visually striking forms of fan engagement that centre on conventions is 'cosplay', abbreviated from 'costume play', which is a kind of performance in which individuals dress up as characters from existing media (including comics, animation, film, and TV). Cosplayers typically make and design their own costumes, selecting on the basis of their level of engagement with individual characters, including their values and behaviours, and their actual appearance. This practice allows for considerable flexibility of representation. Joel Gn notes that

> For the cosplayer, it is not only the modification of the text that is liberating (or, in other instances, subversive), but also the consumption of the image that becomes a pleasurable, embodied experience. In addition, cosplay can take the form of 'crossplay', in which the socially accepted gender of the subject is at odds with that of the character.

> (2011: 584)

Cosplay is a largely misunderstood fan activity, attracting derogatory comments such as: 'it's just kids dressing up' or 'adults shouldn't be acting like this'. The level of engagement with the fan text is much higher than with other kinds of fan activity since it involves the long and often highly skilled design and creation of the costume, which must convey a sense of authenticity, and the wearing of it as part of a performance in itself. The fact that all this is intimately absorbed into the body of the cosplayer makes this a deeply personal expression of fandom, hereby establishing an intimate relationship between fan and character: 'Through the acts of constructing and wearing a costume, the fan constructs his or her identity in relation to fiction and enacts it' (Lamerichs, 2010: 7). Figure 4.4 shows a female cosplayer at San Diego Comic Con; she is dressed as the Marvel character 'Scarlet Witch'. Many cosplayers have professionally shot images, such as this one, to show off their costumes and to distribute at conventions. Cosplay gives fans a multi-levelled expression of their fandom because not only does it reward artistic skill and encourage community with other cosplayers, both online and at conventions, but it also gives fans a space to embody the characters that shape their

Figure 4.4 An example of cosplay, 'Scarlet Witch' by Kaitlyn Gilman (2019).

reading experiences. As Lamerichs puts it, 'Cosplay is an excellent example of how fans actualize fiction in daily life and identify with it, and thus it helps us understand the constitution of fan identity' (2010: 7).

Participation and creative engagement

For many fans, a key element of their association with a certain form, text, or creator is being able to develop their own responses to what they are consuming. This involves going beyond the product offered by the publisher or creator, and allowing the consumer to engage in artistic continuations, subversions, responses, and backstories. It can also involve adding to the interpretive conversations by offering new and innovative readings of existing texts. In this way, the individual fan contributes reflexively to the formation of the product, extending its range and appeal in a way that can allow other fans to pick it up and develop it further. Henry Jenkins describes this process by categorising fans as people who transform their consumption 'into some kind of cultural activity, by sharing feelings and thoughts about the [...] content with friends, by joining a "community" of other fans who share common interests' (2006: 41). Jenkins lays out the defining characteristics of participatory culture in a White Paper on media and education. Such fandom certainly blurs the boundaries between creator, provider, and consumer. Such cultures, he argues, have relatively low barriers to artistic expression and engagement; they demonstrate strong support for sharing creations with the community; they offer an informal mentorship model to pass information and experience to novices; and they provide a general and communal sense of the importance of the individual's contribution at the same time that they offer a sense of social connection and reciprocal socialisation (Jenkins, 2009: xi–xii). He goes on to add that key forms of participation include: affiliations (members of online communities, including Facebook groups, subreddits, and fora), expressions (creating new forms, including fan fiction writing, zines, and film-making), collaborative problem-solving (working together to gather existing and develop new knowledge, such as through Wikipedia), and circulation (shaping the flow of media through media as podcasting, blogging). At one level, this points to a process of democratisation, but at the other extreme it provides an opportunity for the commercial supplier to suck the reader into helping to construct and revitalise a particular text.

Jenkins perceives fans as groups that actively interact with their object of choice *against* any institutional or canonical standard for engagement:

> Unimpressed by institutional authority and expertise, the fans assert their own right to form interpretations, to offer evaluations, and to construct cultural canons. Undaunted by traditional conceptions of literary and intellectual property, fans raid mass culture, claiming its material for their own use, reworking them as the basis for their own cultural creations and social interactions. [...] Fans actively assert their mastery over the mass-produced texts which provide the raw materials for their own cultural productions and the basis for their social interaction.
>
> (1992: 18, 23)

Conceptualising fans in this way gives them considerable agency, with fan-created cultural productions existing in self-governed communities that accord them canonical status and reading them as ciphers of both the individual's and the community's desires.

Participatory cultures of comics have existed for many decades, although the different types of (and fora for) engagement and participation have changed and developed in response to the availability of different communication technologies. Matthew Pustz recognises the importance of pen and paper in the pre-internet era of comics discussions. He writes:

> Letters pages and fanzines were crucial sites for fan interaction and expression in the era before the internet. For decades, mainstream and even many alternative or independent comic books featured regular columns for letters to the editor. Fans wrote letters to comment on stories, correct

mistakes, provide interpretations, or even respond to other fans. The best letters pages gave correspondents – many of whom were very well known in the fan community – a chance to share ideas or debate various theories about their favourite characters.

(Pustz, 2017: 269)

Letters pages did not just print prose communication received from fans, but occasionally also printed fan-submitted artwork and opened communication channels with receptive artists and writers. Of course, conversations could only progress as fast as each comics issue was published. In some cases (including my own) dedicated readers may only have had a letter accepted for print after many attempts. In addition, which letters were published was entirely the decision of the publishers and constrained by space. The rise of internet fora and discussion boards has moved these conversations away from print, opening the scope for wider involvement and drastically reducing response times.

Explicitly artistic engagement with comics media, making creative things that derive directly from the aesthetics of the form, is a popular choice for fans. This can include visual, audio-visual, or textual arts. Prior to the development of modern copyright regulations, plots and characters were freely used and reused and there was no fear of recrimination simply because these elements were nobody's property. Copyright legislation first appeared in the UK in 1710, in an act with the wonderfully wordy title 'An Act for the Encouragement of Learning, by vesting the Copies of Printed Books in the Authors or purchasers of such Copies, during the Times therein mentioned'. The passing of legislation is always a slow process, and even in the twenty-first century, copyright law is complex. The many layers of intellectual property permissions, public domain issues, and fair use conditions mean that such cases, when taken to court, are not easy to resolve and can result in long, drawn-out legal battles that then lead to revisions to statutes. As such, fandoms generally seek to avoid this complexity. As Kristina Busse writes,

Traditionally, media fandom has tried to stay under the radar of the producers and actors and not to profit from any of their fan works. Both rules were created to protect the uncertain legal status of fan works and until recently were not challenged. As a result, transgressing these rules upsets large sections of that specific fan community. Selling one's fan fiction, for example, tends to result in immediate outcries and criticism as well as public mocking and shaming.

(Busse, 2013: 85)

In the vast majority of cases, this is never an issue because fan creation is not for commercial gain but remains within the community, though some do post their work to non-community-linked websites and social media.

Let us turn first to fan fiction which, at a basic level, is fictional prose written by fans, incorporating characters, locations, or other information from a media source. The level of complication of the form depends on which elements of fandom and fan creation are utilised in determining its classification. As Hellekson and Busse observe:

If the term requires an actual community of fans who share an interest, then Sherlock Holmes would easily qualify as the first fandom, with fan-written Holmes pastiches serving as the beginnings of fan fiction. [...] If we look at it as a (sometimes purposefully critical) rewriting of shared media, then media fan fiction, starting in the 1960s with its base in science fiction fandom and its consequent zine culture, would start fan fiction proper.

(2014: 6)

As a distinct, named expression of fandom, the matter of interaction between an original text and what it is subsequently used to generate has become more popular since the advent of the internet. In the early years of the internet, group mailing lists provided a nexus for writers of fan fiction to come together. The form received a boost in 1998 with the launch of FanFiction.Net, which had no regulations regarding who could join or what they could post, with subsections to accommodate all kinds of fandom. This is still the most popular site for posting fan fiction, with approximately 150 million unique visitors per month. The second most popular site is Wattpad. com, with 134 million unique monthly views. Though it is difficult to know for certain, because of the inherent anonymity involved in any website registration, fan fiction has generally been thought of as written and consumed by women.

According to Bacon-Smith, fan fiction 'fill[s] the need of a mostly female audience for fictional narratives that expand the boundary of the official source products offered on the television and movie screen [or comics page]' (2000: 112–113). The opportunity to push the narratives of a media text into previously untouched areas, be they romantic pairings, shifting gender or sexual identities of characters, or story arcs, gives fans of all identities and backgrounds the opportunity to become a part of their favourite media. Though the field has increased in diversity in recent years, mainstream comics especially have not been known for their inclusion of a fair representation of social demographics. Fan fiction gives female and LGBT+ fans opportunities to make themselves characters. More importantly, the results are now filtering into the canon, with more characters and story arcs that present a nuanced and non-tokenistic representation of these demographic groups. Rebecca Black sees FanFiction.Net and other fora for storytelling as 'affinity spaces [,] organised around a common endeavour or interest rather than temporal or spatial proximity' (2007: 289). As such they are 'able to span differences in gender, race, class, age, ability, and education level' (Black, 2007: 289). These groups do not mimic the demographic of most participants' immediate environments, and they can therefore be a hugely enriching experience. In this way, fan fiction can be both collective and connective.

Just as FanFiction.Net publishes millions of items of fan-composed writing and receives millions of views, DeviantArt acts as a cognate location for visual art, with approximately 120 million unique views monthly. Users can post visual art in any form, including photography, traditional and mixed media, and videography. Founded in 2000, the site allows users ('artists') to upload and share their work, comment on the works of others, and form smaller groups within the website, many of which are dedicated to discussion of specific fan media or fan expressions. As with all fan creativity, the issue of copyright looms in the background, but, for the most part, those who post their work to DeviantArt and similar sites do not seek to make a profit and so remain unaffected. This is also the case with those who create fan comics, who take the original characters of comics series and re-imagine them in their own work, sometimes using similar artistic styles and techniques, and who sometimes purposely redraw them in different styles in order to highlight the artist's own skills and imagination. Fan art is often used for comedy purposes or to highlight issues within the specific comics story world or industry. In the case of The Hawkeye Initiative (THI), it can also be both. THI was set up in 2012 in response to sexualised depictions of female characters in American mainstream (predominantly superhero) comics, and its mission statement claims that the site 'draw[s] attention to how deformed, hypersexualized, and unrealistically dressed women are drawn in comics' (*THI*, 2012: n.p.). It is often noted that these representations are not recognised as being inherently anatomically ridiculous when performed by female characters; the absurdity becomes apparent only when men are depicted in this way. The character of Hawkeye has become attached to this site because an image of him with Black Widow was among the first to be created. Such fan art does not necessarily take anything away from the individual's enjoyment of the work but does highlight the broader persistent issue of sexism in Comics.

As we have already seen in the scholarship of Paul Lopes mentioned earlier, fan engagement is generally viewed with disdain, because it is associated with low art forms. The issue is, however, often a matter of naming. Fans of all kinds of media focus on the works they enjoy, and they rework, reinterpret, and recreate them in new ways, in new media, and in new contexts. By this reckoning, we might interpret John Everett Millais' painting 'Ophelia' (1852) as Shakespeare fan art or John William Waterhouse's 'The Lady of Shalott' (1888) as Tennyson fan art. The main difference is that both paintings are housed in a major art gallery (Tate Britain), and they engage with canonical texts. However, my points remain: it is a matter of naming, and it is not a practice that is confined to comics. Some of this can be illustrated with the following case study: a reading of a fan art text that acts as *homage* to an original creation and that reinvigorates our understanding and interpretation of both texts. Elsewhere I have discussed the Comic Book Resources website art challenges, which emphasised on their blog that 'Comics Should Be Good' (Earle, 2017). One artist responded to the topic 'What if?' with 'What if Picasso drew the X-Men?'. The result was a reworking of Picasso's 1937 masterpiece 'Guernica' which is itself an example of non-representational art, substituting various members of the X-Men characters for Picasso's original figures. The artist, Cynthia Sousa, posted the work on her DeviantArt page, and feedback was divided between praise for her technique and criticism of her 'appropriation' of high art. 'X-Men Guernica' retains the shape of the original but uses eight X-Men instead of anonymous faces, while both the shape and style, as well as the symbolism, are comparable. Stan Lee was heavily influenced by the Civil Rights Movement when developing the X-Men in the 1960s, and I have suggested that 'the basic narrative that runs through all X-Men comics is of the mutants working to coexist peacefully with humans'. Indeed, while Picasso's focus is the bombing of Guernica and depicts a strategic attack on a specific group, the Basque people, Sousa's work translates it into an attack on the mutants of Professor X's academy: 'X-Men Guernica' shifts Picasso's work from being an indictment of the violence of the Spanish Civil War (Earle, 2017: 190). This kind of fan art reconfigures an internationally famous painting that speaks directly to the violence, trauma, and futility of war into a poignant reading of a specific comics text and its characters.

Throughout this chapter, I have shown that fandom within comics exists beyond the panel and page. To quote Duffett, 'Fans are networkers, collectors, tourists, archivists, curators, producers and more' (2013: 21). Stereotypes of the hulking, antisocial male fan are *passé*; fans come from all walks of life and demonstrate their fandom in diverse ways. They engage in consumption and creation that are both connective and collective. A large proportion of comics fans are 'active participants in the construction and circulation of textual meanings', and their creative interactions with the form have demonstrable impact on its development (Jenkins, 1992: 24).

5   Journalism

The history of comics in relation to journalism is extensive, as we saw in Chapter 2, and it has grown out of a rich tradition of image-driven satire and political cartooning. This chapter discusses comics in two ways: as a vehicle for socio-political comment that sits alongside more traditional forms of journalism and, conversely, as a journalistic form itself. We will also consider the wider international contexts in which they appear, and we will ask the following question: why do comics and cartoons have the power they do to make certain statements and how is this being mobilised?

Let us begin by discussing what comics journalism is in relation to both comics and journalism, taking a sideways glance at comics in relation to journalism and social comment. Then I will discuss two cases that raise a number of questions concerning ethical questions about the freedom of the press, and the limits that should or should not be placed upon it in order to prevent causing offence to particular sections of the public. These cases are the *Charlie Hebdo* shooting in January 2015 and the *Jyllands-Posten* Muhammad cartoon controversy in 2005, in relation to issues of free speech and offence. The ease of international connectivity through the medium of advanced communication technology means that a message (or comic) can be transmitted easily anywhere in the world. It does *not*, however, mean that it will translate easily into another culture or that the ideological distortions that it carries will be understood, agreed with, and accepted in the same way (if at all). This chapter will conclude by giving some consideration to long-form comics journalism, with particular focus on the works of Joe Sacco (who is generally heralded as the creator of the genre), Sarah Glidden, and Guy Delisle. Ultimately, this chapter aims to examine comics both as a medium for social comment and as an agent for change, keeping in mind that such change is not necessarily always positive or, indeed, what we expect.

Let me begin by asking: what is 'comics journalism'? Before we proceed to answer this question, it will be useful to remind ourselves of the definition of journalism. In his 1998 book *The Sociology of Journalism,* Brian McNair describes it as 'any authored text in written, audio or visual form, which claims to be (i.e., is presented to its audience as) a truthful statement about, or record of, some hitherto unknown (new) feature of the actual, social world' (1998: 4). A prominent feature of journalism is its ephemerality in that it responds usually very quickly to current issues, whether they are social, political, or cultural. Comics journalism finds its roots in several non-Comics forms, including traditional prose journalism and 'New Journalism' (see Vanderbeke, 2010). While traditional journalism aimed for objectivity, impartiality, and a narratorial voice that kept the journalist invisible, New Journalism used subjective perspective that privileged 'truth' over facts and often saw the journalism as a 'character' within the piece. Johannes Schmid contends that longer comics journalism that is published as bound books, such as those I will discuss further in the last section of this chapter, 'has much in common with documentary film' (2016: 23). Being visual forms, film and comics are able to work in both realistic and symbolic registers. Nonetheless, Comics is to be distinguished from film in a number of ways. Weber and Rall point out that

> One might argue that the conventions of comics and the conventions of journalism are totally different. Comics consist of fiction, drama, emotions, exaggerations and funny pictures. In contrast, journalism is based on facts, news and reality, with the associated values: accuracy in reporting,

truthfulness, credibility, public accountability, fairness, impartiality and objectivity.

(2017: 378)

In his definition of Comics journalism, Williams discusses the use of multiple registers and the relationship between word and image. He describes the multiple registers as 'code-switching', further suggesting that this is 'a major strength of comics journalism' (2005: 53). As I demonstrate in this chapter, comics journalism spans a wide range of types of narrative and levels of interaction between creator and subject; a large number of comics journalists focus on human interest pieces, while others are telling powerful, rigorously researched, complex socio-political stories. Williams adds that:

> In comics journalism, more so perhaps than in any other medium, the reporter's role is consistently emphasised. He is often present, not merely as a voice or talking head, but as a moral viewpoint and as a participant in the events described.
> (2005: 55)

This is an issue that we will return to later in this chapter, in relation to Joe Sacco. It is one of the elements that comics journalism has in common with documentary film-making (especially the work of Michael Moore, Louis Theroux, and Morgan Spurlock) and Gonzo journalism (which places the journalist as first-person narrator and privileges emotion and personal experience; the term – and style – was made famous by Hunter S. Thompson).

Comics and journalism co-exist not only in the editorial pages of newspapers or in self-contained codices, but also online through social media including Facebook and Instagram, and in publications such as *The Nib* (which is published both in hard copy and online) and the now-discontinued *Symbolia* (which was published online between 2012 and 2015); Weber and Rall describe *Symbolia* as 'the first multimedia magazine of illustrated journalism' (2017: 376). *The Nib*, founded by Matt Bors in 2013, publishes comics that are rigorously researched and make important interventions into contemporary conversations. Topics covered include matters such as left-leaning politics, international relations, the American Presidency, and all manner of contemporary social issues, ranging from racism and the prison–industrial complex to women's healthcare and anti-vaccination. For the founding of *Symbolia* in 2012, co-founder and artist Joyce Rice created an initial statement to explain the reason for the decision to use comics for journalism. Rice used the form to demonstrate what comics journalism does that other types do not. Her argument pivots on a belief that 'art = access', a point that is located at the heart of the ethos of many creators, especially those who work on non-fictional, journalistic, and educational comics. As we have already seen, Comics can make complex narratives and information accessible to a wide range of readers and can reach audiences that other forms generally do not. The visual nature of the form can cut across language and education barriers. But, sometimes, this level of accessibility *can* be an issue, especially when the images and representations are culturally and politically charged. Let us turn to two examples of Comics (more specifically political cartooning) that caused considerable controversy and led to international repercussions for the publications and deadly consequences for some of the artists involved and for their killers.

Graphic controversies, political comics, and social unrest

On 7 January 2015, at around 11am, two armed men entered the Paris offices of the French satirical magazine *Charlie Hebdo*. They shot twenty-three people, killing twelve and seriously injuring eleven. Among those killed were the director of publication, Charb (Stéphane Charbonnier), several cartoonists, and two police officers, one of whom was Charb's bodyguard. The gunmen, brothers Saïd and Chérif Kouachi, claimed that they belonged to the Islamist terror organisation Al-Qaeda, which quickly claimed responsibility for the attack. On leaving the scene, the gunmen said, 'we have avenged the Prophet Muhammad, we killed Charlie Hebdo' (Sage, 2015: n.p.). Following the shooting, the brothers escaped but were eventually killed by police after a shoot-out on 9 January.

The international response came almost immediately. On 11 January, forty world leaders and over two million people attended a rally to promote national solidarity in Paris. A further four million people demonstrated solidarity across Europe. Outpourings of support for the magazine came from across much of the world, and the slogan *Je Suis Charlie* (I am Charlie) became an all-encompassing statement that expressed support and solidarity for the satirical comic and the victims, as well as a popular hashtag on Twitter. In predominantly Muslim countries, the response was divided between those groups who expressed sympathy with the victims and those who supported the actions of the gunmen. The magazine did not cease publication, and the following issue print reached 7.95 million copies in six languages; previously, a typical run had been around 60,000 and exclusively in French. Cartoonists responded with their pens and the adage 'the pen is mightier than the sword' became a common theme in editorial cartoons for several weeks after the attacks. All manner of outlets, from *The Daily Show with Jon Stewart* to *The Simpsons,* made public statements. The closing image of *The Simpsons* episode broadcast that week was a sketch of baby Maggie Simpson, styled after Eugène Delacroix's 'Liberty Leading the People', holding a *Je Suis Charlie* sign. Albert Uderzo, the creator of *Astérix*, who had retired in 2011, came out of retirement to create a single graphic statement, and the Empire State Building in New York was lit up in the colours of the French *Tricolore*, as was the National Gallery in London, among others.

These attacks were seen not just as a horrifying act of public violence, but also as a challenge to the freedom of expression of the press. The French constitution enshrines *Laïcité* (the separation of Church and State and removal of religion from all governmental processes) as a core value, along with the tripartite motto of the French Republic, *Liberté, Égalité, Fraternité*. Andre Oboler writes:

> *Charlie Hebdo* was known to be a highly controversial satirical publication that regularly mocked sources of power in society, including religion. This mocking was often extreme. The paper's slogan, 'dumb and nasty' (*'bête et méchant'*), came

from a letter of complaint sent in the 1960s […] *Charlie Hebdo's* often distasteful attacks on religion in general, and on Islam in particular, are seen as continuing the tradition of *laïcité*. The threats, and then attack, by those seeking to prevent this mockery of their religion, is therefore seen by many in France as an external attack on core French values.

(2015: n.p.)

Many opinion pieces written about the attacks centred on this issue: that freedom of expression must necessarily include freedom to offend. Media historian Simon Dawes went further when he claimed that the responses to the attacks were tantamount to 'the fetishisation of free speech' (2015: 2). More recently, Amnesty International suggested that 'the right to freedom of expression applies to ideas of all kinds including those that may be deeply offensive' (2018: n.p.). This statement builds on words from the European Court of Human Rights that the rights of free speech 'are the demands of pluralism, tolerance and broad-mindedness without which there is no "democratic society"' (2006: n.p.).

The *Charlie Hebdo* shootings are an extreme example of many recent events that have been triggered, or exacerbated, by cartoons. Ten years prior to the Paris attacks, in 2005, the Danish daily newspaper *Jyllands-Posten* published twelve images of the Muslim prophet Muhammad. The decision, taken by culture editor Flemming Rose, centred on a children's book about the life of Muhammad by Danish author Kåre Bluitgen, who had considerable difficulty in finding an illustrator to work with. The images were accompanied by a short essay, written by Rose, where he wrote:

The modern secular society is dismissed by some Muslims. They demand special treatment when they insist on special consideration of their religious feelings. This is incompatible with secular democracy and freedom of speech, where one should be ready to stand scorn, mockery and ridicule. This is certainly not always very sympathetic or nice to look at, but this is irrelevant in the context.

(2005: n.p.)

It is impossible to think that Rose did *not* anticipate the backlash that his article might provoke; in a later article, he described it as 'the worst foreign policy crisis in Denmark since the Second World War' (2005: 17). The socio-political ramifications of the publication had far-reaching consequences, and soon after eleven ambassadors from Muslim-majority countries requested a meeting with the Danish Prime Minister. At least 50 international news outlets republished some or all the cartoons, and Muslim fundamentalists responded by issuing fatwas against the illustrators. Danish products were boycotted, and several countries in the Middle East held demonstrations and burned the Danish flag. The violence reached its peak in 2006 with attacks on Danish embassies in four countries and the deaths of several hundred people in riots and targeted attacks across the world. In 2008, three people were arrested for planning to assassinate Kurt Westergaard, who had drawn the infamous 'bomb cartoon' depicting Muhammad wearing a turban in which a bomb, with lit fuse, is nestled and fizzing. Westergaard still remains in hiding some twelve years after the event.

Few of the statements adopted the familiar form of multi-panel comics, preferring either the single-image graphic cartoon style or simply appearing as a prose response. However, on Friday, 9 January 2015, *The Guardian* published a short comic by Joe Sacco, titled 'On Satire: a response to the Charlie Hebdo attacks'. Figure 5.1 shows the first tier of the comic, in which Sacco explains his reaction to the news of the attacks and the sadness of hearing of the death of '[his] tribe' (2015: n.p.). Sacco goes on to explain that 'tweaking the noses of Muslims' and Charlie Hebdo's brand of satire are, in his view, 'vapid'. While acknowledging that in a democracy there remains the right to offend, he asks his readers to consider why we hold so strongly to this right, rather than expressing a greater awareness of our place within the wider global society and showing a more acute sensitivity to its various pressures. In his short strip, Sacco draws a number of what we would readily concede are stereotypical offensive images: for example, a black man eating a banana in a tree, a Jewish man counting money while standing in entrails, and himself being beheaded by a hooded swordsman in a desert. He pinpoints the

Figure 5.1 'On Satire' by Joe Sacco (2015).

offence these images carry, and he demonstrates his own freedom to reiterate the process: he asks: 'can I play this game too? Sure, I could draw a black man falling out of a tree with a banana in his hand… in fact, I just did'. And he uses these images to affirm the right to, as he puts it, 'take the piss' (2015: n.p.). The juxtaposition of intentionally offensive images and critical, reflective commentary demonstrates the possibilities that comics possess to make bold statements. The images displayed without verbal captions would offend; the words themselves add a layer of commentary and explanation that shows us how these images work to offend and why the results are deeply problematic.

Why, then, are comics and cartoons able to make statements that have *such* a profound effect on large numbers of people from diverse communities? In the cases of the two examples I have discussed, it should be remembered that many practising Muslims refrain from visually representing the prophet Muhammad, unlike in the case of Christian art that reproduces and illustrates iconographic representations of all kinds of the Christian narrative. For Muslims, the refusal to represent the prophet is called Aniconism, which is defined as the avoidance of visual representation of sentient beings. This extends beyond Aniconism and into the wider world of graphic images. There are three distinct issues at play here: immediacy, transmission, and silence. Image-driven content provokes an immediate response and many scholars have written about the notion of effective and affective immediacy. For example, Nicholas Mirzoeff writes that

> The very element that makes visual imagery of all kinds distinct from texts [is] its sensual immediacy. This is not at all the same thing as simplicity, but there is an undeniable impact on first sight that a written text cannot replicate.
>
> (2008: 15)

Of course, it is entirely possible to react emotionally to, say, a written description of the bombing of Guernica in 1937, but it will have a different effect on the reader compared to that generated by a viewing of Picasso's excruciating painting of the same event: the impact that the painting has is more immediate than the text description would suggest. A good deal of this kind of criticism and theory on this topic has emerged from the analysis of the photographic image but this also holds true for comics, especially short editorial and single-panel works. When we look at a comic or image, particularly those that contain humans, we can recognise it and form a connection with it, but this is also the case with non-human representations. How many of us have laughed at, or felt sympathy for, an animal in a comic strip or editorial cartoon? We recognise some modicum of humanity and respond to it considerably faster than when reading text. Daniel Kahneman explains this in terms of the different processing points within the brain. Visual information bypasses the (slower) visual cortex and goes directly to the amygdala for (fast) threat assessment. This saves a few hundredths of a second, which may improve chances for survival and, thus, be an evolutionary advantage (Kahneman, 2012: 301). Though we are no longer on the lookout for predators who are searching for their next meal, our brains still process this information as if we were. That punch to the gut you feel looking at an emotive comic shares its neurological heritage with 'fight or flight' threat assessment.

Another important issue involves the question of transmission. According to James Der Derian, 'time displaces space as the most strategic "field"' when it comes to the movement of visual communication: those who can disseminate their visuals fastest take the lead' (1992: 134). The internet age allows us to contact billions of people in seconds; social media allow us to share images at the click of a mouse, and the result is that dissemination can be almost instantaneous. This can in theory be said of text just as well as of image, but the clear difference between the two, especially once international borders are crossed, is that images can be immediately recognised by everyone even though their wider resonances might not necessarily be 'understood'. The Muhammad cartoons were received with quiet protest by the Muslim community of Denmark, and under normal circumstances there might have been no further repercussions. The Danish legislation on freedom of expression, was, it seems, understood and accepted, despite disagreement among some. It was only when these graphic images were transmitted internationally that the issue escalated. This suggests that *where* cartoons are seen can drastically change their meaning. Habitually, we read and interpret what we see on social media or image-sharing sites in different ways compared with something that is posted on a website of a major newspaper or political commentary hub. These publication contexts are very easy to overlook in transmission. The Muhammad cartoons were initially published in a centre-right newspaper in a democratic and politically open country, in stark contrast to the context of the millions of individuals who saw them on unregulated internet fora and social media.

Another important element that we need to consider is silence. W.J.T. Mitchell suggests that the visual cannot speak itself, but that its voice is provided by the viewer and that it is only in relation to a person that it gains 'voice':

> Images are not words. It is not clear that they actually 'say' anything. They may show something, but the verbal message or speech act has to be brought to them by the spectator, who projects a voice into the image, reads a story into it, or deciphers a verbal message. Images are dense, iconic (usually) visual symbols that convey non-discursive, non-verbal

information that is often quite ambiguous with regard to any statement.

(2005: 140)

Comics is primarily, but not exclusively, visual and often contains words in the form of captions or speech-bubbles but, as I have stated repeatedly, is ultimately driven by image. Like all other visual representations, comics are built on frameworks of culturally coded signs. In Chapter 1, I discussed the ways in which jokes in comic strips target those readers who have an intimate familiarity with the discursive field in which the joke is positioned. Mitchell argues that this information shared between the reader and the representation is precisely what gives the image its semantic vitality and that without it, the representation is meaningless. Similar observations are often made about photographic images, and they occur frequently in the analytical discourse of photo-journalism where, according to Campbell, they are 'made available with an intertextual setting – where title, caption and text surround the particular content of the photograph – [and] they are read within an historical, political and social context' (2004: 62–63). Perhaps, then, this is less about the silence of the comic itself and more about the voices of interpretation: in such cases the silence is augmented by requiring the reader to examine 'the ways in which images themselves may function as communicative acts' in order to produce 'an analysis of how meaning is conveyed' and of how images 'impact on different audiences' (Williams, 2003: 527). In such instances, images such as the Muhammad cartoons signify differently to different viewers depending upon their religious, social, and cultural proclivities.

Let us now examine two specific examples of political cartoons and comics from very different eras and contexts in order to illustrate these issues. On 9 May 1754, the *Pennsylvania Gazette* published 'Join or die', a cartoon that commented on colonial union in the emerging US. The visual image is a woodcut, attributed to Benjamin Franklin, which shows a snake cut into eight segments, each labelled with the initials of one of the American colonies (Figure 5.2). It was accompanied by an editorial, penned by Franklin, which discussed the 'disunited state' of the colonies and emphasised strongly the merits of

Figure 5.2 'Join or Die' by Benjamin Franklin (attrib.) (1754).

colonial unity. The cartoon became a popular symbol during the American Revolutionary War. It made a far greater impression and lasted much longer in the public memory than Franklin's actual words. The cartoon played on the prevailing belief at the time that a snake that had been cut into pieces would be healed if the pieces were put back together before the sun set. Opinion on its meaning was, of course, divided. The Patriots, who supported the new American republic, saw it as an image of connection, vigilance, and strength; the Loyalists, who advocated allegiance to Britain, read the cartoon in the light of the biblical serpent that was a manifestation of evil deceit and treachery. In itself, the image is very simple. The linework is bold and unfussy; the wording is sparse. And yet the opposing messages it was thought to contain were quickly and effectively transmitted. If we consider the print culture of the time, we can clearly see why this image looks as it does. It would not have been expensive or difficult to reproduce – an eighteenth-century version of today's highly shareable memes. It is a cartoon that focuses upon separation and division, mobilising the visual form to force the viewer to envisage the dismembered colonies and instilling a desire to mentally reconstruct them. The representation, therefore, either became an image of the desirability of separation, or the image of union, depending on which side of the political divide the reader happened to be.

In 2019, political comics platform *The Nib* commissioned a series of short 'response' comics to current socio-political issues, and they were published on Instagram and on *The Nib's* website. UK Comics Laureate Hannah Berry created a four-panel comic as her response to the UK's decision to depart from the EU ('Brexit'), highlighting the familial discord caused by her partner's French nationality and her father's British 'leave' vote (Figure 5.3). Berry used a different image of disconnection from Franklin's, which was a literal cutting of the English Channel with a pair of scissors representing a stark visual separation of the UK from the EU. We can clearly see what Berry had in mind: Brexit would mean a complete cutting off, an amputation, for her family and for the UK. In contrast, someone who supported

Figure 5.3 'Brexit' by Hannah Berry (2019).

Berry's father's political position and voted 'leave' in the 2016 public referendum would not regard separation as an amputation but a reclaiming of national sovereignty for the UK. Both Berry and Franklin, though they are separated by almost two and a half centuries in time, deploy the techniques of Comics to represent political unity and disunity. Indeed, although they were created centuries apart, both images are designed to make an immediate impact in that they both attract the viewer's attention immediately, and appeal directly to both sides of the political arguments at whose services they are deployed.

Comics journalism: three key figures

Joe Sacco (1960–) is one of the most frequently mentioned names in comics journalism. Sacco trained as a journalist at the University of Oregon, wanting to write hard-hitting, affective journalism. After leaving the university, he began as a guidebook writer in Malta, creating and drawing comics as a hobby. After returning to the US, Sacco began to work for a range of comics publications, including the satirical *Portland Permanent Press* and *The Comics Journal*. However, what consolidated Sacco's reputation as a leading figure in the development of comics journalism began with *Palestine*, which was serialised from 1993 to 1995 and published as a trade paperback in 1996. *Palestine* is a collection of narratives and travelogues from Sacco's time in Israel and Palestine in 1991, and several of them are retellings of stories he was told by Palestinians and Israelis. This collection won an American Book Award in 1996 and heralded the beginning of a new, dynamic use of Comics as a vehicle for journalism and investigative reportage. Sacco returned to the region for his 2009 graphic novel *Footnotes in Gaza* that follows the artist's investigations into two massacres, at Khan Younis and Rafah, in 1956. The story is assembled through interviews with residents and official source material, all of which is developed alongside contemporaneous events, including the death of American activist Rachel Corrie. Sacco's comics journalism could be divided into two categories: the first is his work on the Middle East, while the second focuses on the Balkans. Both *Safe Area Goražde* (2000) and *The*

Fixer: A Story from Sarajevo (2003) focus on the impact of this intensely complex conflict from a single, narrow perspective. He extended this in 2005, when he published *War's End: Profiles from Bosnia 1995–96*, a project funded by the prestigious Guggenheim Fellowship. From this, we can conclude that Sacco's close association with Comics had now begun to be taken seriously as a form of journalism.

Sacco's work is ground-breaking because of the ways in which he adapts his skills as an artist and elides them with his journalistic training. His creations are rigorously researched, but more importantly than this for our purposes, he mobilises the mechanics of the Comics form to ensure that his work will appeal to the reader on several levels. He takes complex, convoluted geopolitical conflicts and extracts from them the stories that humanise the conflict so that readers can connect on an emotional level with the stories themselves. This is in addition to the factual details of the conflicts he describes, as Bake and Zohrer observe:

> Besides the comics-immanent possibilities Sacco uses in order to tell the truth, he also breaks with expectations and draws on techniques that are more conventional in science, news journalism, or NGO human rights reporting for that matter, using, for example, footnotes, quotes and geographic maps.
> (2017: 86)

Gilbert and Keane compare Sacco to 'foreign correspondents or documentary film-makers' insofar as they 'share many of their functions and have adopted a similar ethos' (2015: 239). Benjamin Woo argues that Sacco does not interview 'notable people' (2010: 173); Hillary Chute counters by writing that 'Sacco visualises history based on oral testimonies he solicits from others, in a sense producing an archive from non-archived material' (2011: 108). If journalism is based on revealing something 'hitherto unknown', then Sacco's archive-building does exactly this, giving voice to the unspoken experiences of ordinary individuals and communities.

Sacco is present within his comics in that, as Woo suggests, 'he draws himself into the background as a near-constant figure whose presence dismantles the conceit of detached journalistic objectivity' (2010: 75). The author avatar he employs is heavily caricatured (his features are exaggerated) and wears blank glasses, allowing the reader to project themselves onto the character, a technique that will be further discussed in Chapter 6. Sacco has said that 'some people have told me that hiding my eyes makes it easier for them to put themselves in my shoes, so I've kind of stuck with it. I'm a nondescript figure; on some level, I'm a cipher' (qtd in Cooke, 2009: n.p.). He acts as a witness, watching the events around him without interacting, but rather bearing witness and reporting. Moreover, in placing himself in the action, Sacco shows how he is involved in the creation of the story he is writing. The narrative is based on real events and the accounts of witnesses, but it is also an artefact, something that he is creating from his own perspective, and he is 'concerned with his own entanglement in the material he depicts' (Salmi, 2016: 8).

Unlike some other comics journalists, Sacco draws directly from his own experiences of the specific location he is describing. Kenan Koçak writes:

> Sacco argues that in order to recreate a specific time, place and situation, a comics journalist should draw in a realistic, down-to-earth fashion. This precept is observed by nearly all comics journalists because even those such as Joe Kubert and Kemal Gökhan Gürses, who draw places they have not visited, research photographs, films, documents and others' drawings to create the exact environment.
>
> (2017: 179)

This is not to disparage those who do not write from direct experience, but it does speak to the specific power and influence of Sacco's work. Unlike those who are first and foremost comics artists, and whose primary focus is on the 'comics' part of comics journalism, Sacco's skills as a journalist occupy an equal status with his art. Rosenblatt and Lunsford write, 'More than any other creator of comics reportage, Sacco's work is closer to traditional journalistic practices, and more than any other creator, Sacco self-consciously redefines journalism for the comic book medium' (2010: 69). His work gives voice to individuals whose stories have remained out of the public arena, and opens up this type of journalism to a wider audience. The real aim of Sacco's work is, as Rebecca Scherr writes, 'to rethink his own notions of prejudice and pain, and to convince others to do the same' (2013: 19).

Sarah Glidden (1980–) is another American artist, but one whose work, while clearly comics journalism, is markedly different from Sacco's. Originally from Boston, she studied Art at Boston University and began making comics in 2006, while living at Flux Factory, an artist collective in New York. She has written two long-form comics and a series of shorter pieces for online and print publications. Glidden self-published a series of mini-comics about her 2007 trip to Israel on a 'Birthright Israel' tour, which won a 2008 Ignatz Award for 'New Talent'. She developed these mini-comics into her first book, *How to Understand Israel in 60 Days or Less* (2010), and she describes her experience learning about the history and politics of Israel, reflecting on her own identity as a secular, liberal, Jewish American. Her work is distinctly autobiographical in tone, and she focuses on her own experiences, both on the tour itself and on what she learned about both Israel and her own attitude toward it. Her second book, *Rolling Blackouts: Dispatches from Turkey, Syria, and Iraq* (2016), recounts a trip to the Middle East, when she was accompanied by two freelance journalists who were reporting on the region's refugee crisis.

In contrast to Sacco, Glidden does not work in a strictly journalistic style: she draws images *of* the journalists, but she does not draw images *as a* journalist. Her work is more about reporting on the creation of journalistic responses to an event or, in the case of *Rolling Blackouts*, its aftermath, and allowing her work to reflect on the issues inherent in journalism as a practice. In *Rolling Blackouts*, Glidden accompanies Sarah Stuteville and Alex Stonehill, two journalists who founded *The Seattle Globalist*, and Dan O'Brien, a former Marine. Their aim was to collect personal and record personal experiences and testimonies and to weave together the untold stories of what it was like living in a conflict zone. Rather than writing about the events as they were

happening, Stuteville and Stonehill aimed to examine their aftermath – what remains once soldiers and their military equipment
have left. Glidden's role was to capture the way this kind of journalism works and to try to represent the processes that under-
pinned the images and narratives. As a review published on the
website of the British weekly newspaper *The Observer* stated at
the time:

> Glidden's book only explains what it can show with real
> events. There's no pages breaking down the pieces of the
> crafts as an abstraction, such as: 'how an interview works',
> 'how to find good sources' or 'fact-checking testimonials'.
> Everything she wants us to see, she shows through actual
> events that happened on the trip.
>
> (Dale, 2016: n.p.)

The book is perhaps most notable for the ways in which it
makes the reporting process itself transparent; indeed, not only
does Glidden show how her journalist accomplices find and
collect information from their sources, but she also shows the
relationships that form inside the group, illuminating various
discussions on arising ethical questions and on other aspects of
reportage. Because of the complex and politically charged subject matter, there are many aspects of the book that are controversial. Glidden's depiction of interviews with Kurdish and Iraqi
individuals throughout the book tries to show that their speech
is being translated by another person in the room. She does
this by overlapping their speech bubbles in an aim to represent
graphically the number of voices involved in these exchanges.
For example, in a panel showing a Kurdish woman whose speech
is represented in her native language, the bubble will be almost
entirely obscured by another, overlapping bubble, containing
the English translation. Glidden has been praised for this visual
descriptor of translation, and the book is about giving a voice
to those who have been hitherto ignored in major international
conflicts or whose voices have been silenced by powerful forces
who have dominated the airwaves. The obscuring or silencing
of voices is even more politically offensive when we consider

that many of those silenced in this way are female, while the translators who mediate their voices are mostly male.

Glidden is aware of these issues, and her presence within the text as observer and recorder allows her space to comment on the issues of representation within the work itself. In an interview with Tom Spurgeon, she revealed that:

> With journalism you have to accept it's going to be ethically weird. You have to accept with a book like this that you are going to write pages where it's [just people] in a room talking. It's going to be boring for a couple of pages, and that's okay.
>
> (Spurgeon, 2016: n.p.)

Despite not being trained as a journalist, her understanding of the ethical side of things is solid. Within comics journalism, Glidden's specific position offers new lenses through which we can tell these stories, and she creates a frame that allows both story and form to be critiqued on their own merits.

The final comics artist to be discussed here, Guy Delisle (1966–), creates work that is markedly different from the others mentioned in this chapter. An animator by training, Québécois Delisle worked at animation studios around the world, and his experiences in Asian studios are recorded in two books, *Shenzhen* (2000 [translated to English in 2006]) and *Pyongyang: A Journey in North Korea* (2003 [translated to English in 2004]). His later works derive their narratives from trips to Myanmar and Jerusalem with his wife, who works for the NGO Médecins Sans Frontières. The book that resulted from the Myanmar trip was published as *Burma Chronicles* in 2007 (translated to English in 2008) and the one from the Jerusalem trip was published as *Jerusalem: Chronicles from the Holy City* in 2011 (translated to English in 2012); the latter won the Angoulême International Comics Festival Prize for Best Album in 2012. His latest book, *Hostage* (2016 [translated to English in 2017]), departs from his own experiences and tells the story of Christophe André, a *Médecins Sans Frontières* employee, who was kidnapped in 1997. Whereas Sacco and

Glidden create work that comment and reports directly on events in areas of the world that are noted for their complex histories of conflict and insurgency, Delisle does not. Though he does visit places where there is political unrest and military action (most obviously Israel), his books are perhaps more accurately labelled as travelogues or travel writing. But even then, he does not directly act as a journalist claiming that 'he does not find news, but that news finds him' (Koçak, 2017: 183). Koçak writes:

> In *Jerusalem*, Delisle does not directly write about the conflict between Palestinians and Israelis, he just shows it by drawing armed soldiers, firing guns, shouting people and chaotic streets. With similar intent Sacco constantly keeps streets muddy throughout *Palestine*.
>
> (2017: 178)

These elements are presented without comment and while the conflict is there, there is no clarity of focus. Rather, it is background noise, the socio-cultural canvas onto which Delisle paints his story.

Delisle's work treads a path between the straightforward, factual account of a visitor to a new country and politically and socially charged commentary that the 'facts' might generate. Let us consider his 2003 book *Pyongyang: A Journey in North Korea*. Delisle spent two months in North Korea, working for a French animation studio, which outsourced much of their 'filling in' animation (the animated sequences of movement that are used to knit together longer sequences, designed elsewhere) to a North Korean company. On the face of it, the book follows Delisle as he experiences some of the difficulties in cross-cultural working, as he was being taken on many guided tours to various parts of the city, while staying in an inferior hotel. The drawings he produced are all presented in a simple monochrome style, but there is also biting social critique, beginning when he informs the reader of his choice of reading material for the trip: George Orwell's depiction of the experience of totalitarianism, *Nineteen Eighty-Four*. Throughout the two-month trip, Delisle was able to combine the banality of the job and his experience of residence in a largely empty hotel, with unemotional accounts of cultural tours and trips to national monuments. Throughout he was accompanied by a guide and translator, 'Captain Sin'. One particularly disturbing section recounts Delisle noticing the apparent absence of disabled and elderly people in the streets of Pyongyang. His guide tells him that North Korea has no disabled people: 'All North Koreans are born strong, intelligent and healthy' (Delisle, 2004: 136). A panel depicting Delisle's face – a simple line drawing but clearly displaying incredulity – is what he offers by way of response. This is typical of much of the style of *Pyongyang*; Delisle understands what the Western reader might think of the events and topics being depicted and so he does not feel that additional comment is needed. The image of an incredulous face is enough.

The works of Guy Delisle are not as easily classified as journalistic comics as those of Sacco or Glidden. He does not report on specific events, nor does he position himself explicitly as a journalist. His work fits more neatly into the field of travel literature, which is itself a flexible and contentious genre. For Carl Thompson, travel writing 'encompasses a bewildering diversity of forms, modes, and itineraries' (2011: 1–2). Scholars of the genre often note its inherent classist, and often racist (or at least racially complex), nature. This is most evident in examples of travel narratives from the eighteenth and nineteenth centuries, when the Grand Tour was a popular activity of the privileged classes, but also included diaries of sailors and naturalists (notably Charles Darwin). Others focus on the sociological, geographical, and ethnographic possibilities that these accounts contain, though it is hard to ignore their largely Eurocentric emphasis. Regardless of the writerly – and academic – lenses at play, travel writing is an established, albeit flexible, genre. In placing Delisle's work within this category, two things are being suggested here. First, that we take from his books the story of a journey, with the artist as our guide and representative. Second, that Comics can bring together the nuances and cultural peculiarities of a specific location and display them on the drawn page in ways that are compelling, interesting, and informative. The multi-levelled creation of the image can impart to us particular items of information ('All NK citizens are healthy') but can also provide an accompanying concise social comment such as the silent face at the same time.

The combination of Comics and Journalism brings together two kinds of narrative to provide an effective means of representing complex social and political situations in an unusually vivid way. The sheer economy of the graphic representation combines 'showing' and 'telling', which are the two key components of narrative art.

6   Drawing lives

In 2011, the Angoulême International Comics Festival (*Festival International de la Bande Dessinée d'Angoulême*) was the site of a curious scandal. The source was a young French Comics artist, Judith Forest, who had published her first memoir in 2009. *1hr25* follows her addiction issues, her family relationships, and her experiences of meeting various distinguished comics artists. Forest was interviewed on television and radio, and she had a popular social media presence. Quickly, the suspicions began, especially as many of the people Forest claims to have met did not remember her at all. Many people assumed she did not, in fact, exist and the story was a strange, elaborate hoax. This general air of unease increased with Forest's second graphic memoir, *Momon* (Masquerade), released in 2010. *Momon* is a response to *1hr25*; Forest discusses the success and controversy of the first book and ultimately questions her own existence. *Momon* begins what the editors finished at the Angoulême festival – it *was* a hoax. The woman seen on televised interviews was an actress (Brethes, 2011). What makes this hoax particularly curious is that it does not appear to have been driven by profit and sales. Instead, the aim behind the creation of Forest was to 'generat[e] discussion about the value of authenticity and the limits of autobiographical comics' (Johnson, 2017: 199). The editors, the Belgian press *La Cinquième Couche*, had created something they perceived to be badly written, formulaic, and trite; the Francophone Comics world did not agree, and the fictional Forest became popular. This was not part of the plan but did not affect the aim of the experiment: it did make readers consider the importance of authenticity within autobiography.

Outside of the Comics form, there have been many controversial publications in life writing. One of the most incendiary in the Anglophone world occurred when a skilfully written (if long-winded) memoir of drug addiction and recovery was found to be almost entirely false. James Frey's *A Million Little Pieces* (2003) recounts his experience of drug use, arrest, and rehab, with the addition of some gory and fanciful snippets including a root canal without anaesthetic. The book received a massive boost when Oprah Winfrey discussed it on her show in 2005 and featured Frey as a guest. Unfortunately, in 2006 a long-form article broke down Frey's book piece by piece and revealed it to be a fraud. He was forced to apologise on the Oprah Show, and his publisher offered refunds. Another hoax – one that carries the more horrific burden of being tied to the Shoah – is that of Binjamin Wilkomirski. His memoir *Bruchstücke: Aus Einer Kindheit 1939–1948* (*Fragments: Memories of a Wartime Childhood 1939–1948*) was published in 1995 to huge critical acclaim, winning many major book awards. However, as with Frey, it was not true. Latvian-born Binjamin Wilkomirski was Swiss-born Bruno Grosjean: the vast majority of the memoir, including his reports of events that happened at both Auschwitz and Majdanek, was fabricated. The fact that he chose to adopt the identity of an innocent bound up in the Shoah is unpalatable to many; such lies do not sit well when the experience was a stark reality for so many. Of the book and its autobiographical claims, Maechler writes: 'Once the professed interrelationship between the first-person narrator, the death–camp story he narrates, and historical reality are proved palpably false, what was a masterpiece becomes kitsch' (2001: 81). *Bruchstücke* is not a bad piece of writing; in many ways, it is beautifully constructed and *could* have been considered great as a piece of Shoah fiction. The truth claims removed this option, and, as Maechler states, it becomes kitsch. But, if anything, these scandals only increase our appetite for such stories.

Humans are curious, some many even say nosy, as a species. We want to know things about our fellow humans and actively

seek out this information. Thankfully, humans are also a loqua-
cious species, and we willingly talk about all aspects of our lives
and experiences. Life writing in all its many forms, including
biography, autobiography, memoir, diaries, and letter writing, is
centuries old and part of a venerable tradition of capturing the
human condition in words (or pictures!). Many centuries older
than the novel, this genre finds its roots in two distinct documents
of antiquity: the *Apologia* and the biography. In this sense, the
biography is hard to distinguish from our modern usage of the
word: an account of the lives and actions of notable figures, usually emperors or great statesmen. I doubt whether the authors
of the time thought of their texts as life writing; more likely,
they would have called it history. An *Apologia* is a less common
occurrence in the modern world. The word has nothing to do
with the modern understanding of 'apology'; rather, it is a jus-
tification or defence of one's actions. These two parallel styles
developed into what we now think of as life writing, through
countless iterations and examples from all strata of the social
order. In the eighteenth and nineteenth centuries, the scandalous
(Jean-Jacques Rousseau's *Confessions* [1789]) rubbed shoulders
with the artistic (such as William Hazlitt's *Liber Amoris* [1823])
on bookshelves. This has been the shape of the genre ever since.
As Gillian Whitlock puts it,

> Autobiography is a cultural space where relations between
> the individual and society are thought out intensely and
> experienced intersubjectively; here the social, political, and
> cultural underpinnings of thinking about the self come to
> the surface and are affirmed in images, stories, and legends.
>
> (2007: 11–12)

Modern life writing spans the entire spectrum of human interest,
from celebrities and sports personalities, to political figures and
great thinkers, to tragic life stories and medical narratives.

Of course, with any kind of life writing, we face issues of
representation, 'autobiographical truth' and narration, though
not necessarily on the same level as the works of Forest, Frey,
or Wilkomirski/Grosjean. In her own autobiographical comic,

One! Hundred! Demons! (2002), Lynda Barry uses the term 'Autobiofictionalography', an amusing portmanteau that acknowledges the melting together of truth and fiction that is central to life writing. The issue of 'truth vs. fiction' is an enormous subject and cannot be fully covered in a paragraph, but it bears mentioning because of its importance to the study of life writing in general. We generally assume that, for a piece of life writing to *not* be a work of fiction, basic historical fact must be accurate – dates and locations of birth, life events, and such like. However, Elisabeth El Refaie reminds us that 'it is impossible to draw strict boundaries between factual and fictional accounts of someone's life, since memory is always incomplete and the act of telling one's life story necessarily involves selection and artful construction' (2012: 12). Memory is fallible; our understanding of our lives is governed by perception and subjective viewpoints. Therefore, it is impossible to write something that is 100% accurate on all counts. According to Philippe Lejeune, autobiographical texts involve an implicit understanding between author and reader, which he calls the 'autobiographical pact' (Lejeune, 1989). El Refaie describes this pact as the author 'commit[ing] him- or herself not to some unattainable historical exactitude but to the sincere effort to be as truthful as possible' (2012: 53). Lejeune claims that autobiography 'supposes that there is identity of name between the author, the narrator of the story, and the character who is being talked about' (1989: 12), which 'can only be upheld if the self is construed as a coherent and unified entity' (El Refaie, 2012: 53). We know that this is not how identity works: our selfhood is not fixed, but rather a fluid understanding of self that develops over time.

Comics has not ignored life writing. Instead, the formal aspects of Comics and the arsenal of artistic techniques at hand have been found distinctly able to give shape to intensely personal narratives, with rich focus on individual stories and experiences. 'Autographics', as they are often rendered, are among the most rigorously researched and academically interesting of all areas of Comics Studies. In this chapter, I discuss the history and development of autographics, the myriad issues surrounding author avatars, Graphic Medicine, and end with three case studies.

Ultimately, this chapter suggests reasons for the enduring (and increasing) popularity and success of comics as a form for life writing.

What is autographics?

Put in its simplest terms, autographics is a genre of Comics that contains life writing in all its various guises. The word itself was coined by Gillian Whitlock in a 2006 article. She writes:

> By coining the term 'autographics' for graphic memoir I mean to draw attention to the specific conjunctions of visual and verbal text in this genre of autobiography, and also to the subject positions that narrators negotiate in and through comics.
>
> (2006: 966)

In terms of theme and story construction, there are many similarities between comics and prose life writing. In terms of form and artistic choices, 'comics are capable of demonstrating a broader and more flexible range of first-person narration than is possible in prose' (Versaci, 2012: 36). Versaci adds that, 'while many prose memoirists address the complex nature of identity and the self, comic book memoirists are able to represent such complexities in ways that cannot be captured in words alone' (36). The visual and artistic presentation of autographics does as much to create the story as the plot, story, and characters and, by extension, it guides the reader in their movement through the work. But, as we discussed earlier in this book, the creative choices artists make are bound up in wider concerns including culturally and nationally bound customs of representation (see Chapter 3). Davis positions these wider concerns as being inextricably tied with the individual's story, meaning that these comics 'cannot be read solely as a personal account [as] the cultural connotations of the stories and the narrative choices [...] attest to the complex interweaving of the strategies of meaning' (2005: 270). We cannot remove the social, cultural, national, and ideological from autographics (or any type of life writing across all narrative forms), and we should not seek to. Life writing is about connection – the narrator/author's connection with their world, their past, and their selves. In a narrative form that both privileges the interconnectivity of word and image, although remaining alert to the potential limitations and failures, it is not a stretch to suggest that such formal concerns can be used to represent themes of connection. The form already demands that readers make narrative and hermeneutic connections during the active reading process; mobilising readerly engagement to place the reader in the role of a narrator seeking/creating connection can lead to affective reading experiences and a close relationship between reader and creator to develop empathy and identification. I return to these connections later in the chapter.

In recent decades, autographics has become one of the most widely researched genres of Comics, as well as being the most broadly represented in the canon. Many of the texts that have bolstered Comics' reputation as a narrative form of substance are autographics; many have also been very successful outside of the form itself. Art Spiegelman's rendering of his parents' experience of the Shoah, *Maus* (serialised 1980–1991), won a special Pulitzer Prize in 1992; Alison Bechdel's coming of age story, *Fun Home* (2006), was a finalist for the National Book Critics Circle Award; and *Persepolis,* Marjane Satrapi's 2000 *Bildungsroman*, set against the backdrop of the Islamic Revolution, ranked #5 on Newsweek's list of the ten best fiction books of the decade. In the introduction to his study of Autobiographical Comics, Andrew J. Kunka lists these three works as the recipients of the majority of critical attention in Comics Studies (2017: 2). The wealth of scholarship and popular attention on this very short list of texts may seem to suggest that this particular type of comic is both a recent and a Western phenomenon; in reality, it is neither.

One of the earliest recorded autographics comes from Portugal. Rafael Bordalo Pinheiro, a Portuguese artist and illustrator, had been publishing humorous political caricatures and comics in national newspapers for some time when, in 1881, he created *No Lazareto de Lisboa* (The Lazaretto of Lisbon). This short work contains personal thoughts and events, presented as a series of drawings with captions, in a similar structure to Töpffer's work

Figure 6.1 Cover of *Psit!!!* by Rafael Bordalo Pinheiro (1877).

(see Chapter 2). Figure 6.1 is from the popular Brazilian weekly comic *Psit!!!*, which Bordalo Pinheiro drew during his time in Rio de Janeiro in 1877. It demonstrates the influence of Töpffer and his own development of the Comics form. Unfortunately, Bordalo Pinheiro's example was not taken up widely by Portuguese artists, except for Carlos Botelho. Botelho drew a weekly full-page comic called 'Echoes of the Week' for the humour magazine *Sempre Fixe* between 1928 and 1950 (without a single break). He would weave his own experiences of Lisbon life into the strips, positioning himself as both observer and chronicler of events, while also including a hefty dose of political satire. However, this work received little interest outside of Portugal, and so its cultural weight and influence are relatively low. Despite this, it is crucial to the history of autographics, as it demonstrates that such types of comic were being created in a range of national and social contexts long before typically suggested.

Other early autographics exist in similarly non–Anglophone cultures. Yoshitaka (Henry) Kiyama's *The Four Immigrants Manga* was exhibited in San Francisco in 1927 before being self-published in 1931. Each of the 52 strips is a vignette of an experience of Kiyama and three of his friends, all of them Japanese students who immigrated to San Francisco between 1904 and 1907. Figure 6.2 shows the four friends' arrival in San Francisco, using clear panels and speech bubbles. The rest of the stories cover the arrival, as well as major historical events such as the 1906 San Francisco earthquake, the Panama–Pacific International Exposition of 1915, and the various waves of legislation against Asian immigrations (often nicknamed 'The Yellow Peril'). Another *Manga* artist, Taro Yashima, published two autobiographical works with a similar focus on his personal relationship to major world events. *The New Sun* (1943) describes his life as an anti-war, anti-Imperialist, and anti-militarist Japanese citizen in the 1930s, as well as his wife's imprisonment for the same beliefs, while *The New Horizon* (1947) continues their life post-prison and immigration to the US. A final example from Japan is Yoshiharu Tsuge's 1966 autographics work *Chiko*. Tsuge depicts his life as a struggling artist, dependent on his partner, a

Figure 6.2 From *The Four Immigrants Manga: A Japanese Experience in San Francisco, 1904–1924* by Henry (Yoshitaka) Kiyama, translated by Frederik L. Schodt. © Estate of Yoshitaka Kiyama, Frederik L. Schodt. Used by permission of Stone Bridge Press, Berkeley, California.

bar hostess. His work started the *Watakushi Manga* movement
(I *Manga*) and laid the groundwork for other artists to chronicle their development as an artist in this way, a type of storytelling that shares much with the European tradition of the
Künstlerroman, a narrative tracing the education of an artist (literally 'artist novel'). The relationship between the *Künstlerroman*
and Comics is a strong one, according to Rocío Davis:

> Graphic narratives are highly effective *Künstlerroman* –
> because the subjects of the autobiographical comics are, most
> often, graphic artists themselves. The reader is privileged to
> participate in the performance of both memory and art, and
> the complex interaction between them.

(2005: 269)

Just as the graphic novel is often said to have sprung from
key texts published in 1986 (see Chapter 2), it can be said
that autographics has a 'key year'. In 1972, *Manga* artist Keiji
Nakazawa published a 48-page story titled 'I Saw It', his first-
hand account of the bombing of Hiroshima. The *Manga* is bold
and visceral, depicting the event through the eyes of the child
narrator and changing the parameters for representations of war
in Comics, with the opening of the autobiographical witness
lens. 'I Saw It' was reworked into the longer, fictionalised *Barefoot
Gen*, serialised from 1973 to 1987. In addition, 1972 saw the
publication of Justin Green's *Binky Brown Meets the Holy Virgin
Mary*, a landmark of both medical and confessional memoir,
which I discussed in Chapter 2. It is also the year of the founding
of *Wimmen's Comix*, a female-authored comic (and later artists'
collective) that included work from Aline Kominsky-Crumb,
Diane Noomin, and Trina Robbins (also discussed in Chapter 2).
Jared Gardner writes of the collective that it 'called for a new
approach to personal comix narrative, one that explored the
ways in which collective identities were forged through personal
autobiography and the ways in which personal self-exploration
was strengthened through collective creativity' (2012: 126). It
would not be too bold to suggest that 1972 was the birth year of
Graphic Medicine (though the term itself came later), as well as

the beginning of a greater number of works that saw both sexual and conflict trauma as legitimate themes for autographics. Before turning to the topic of author avatars and self-representation, let us consider the term 'Graphic Medicine'.

Graphic Medicine is a genre of Comics that brings together medicine in all its guises and the Comics form, with special focus on patients and medical memoir. The name itself was coined by Ian Williams, a general practitioner, to encapsulate 'the inter-section between the medium of comics and the discourse of healthcare' (2007: n.p.). While writing his master's dissertation on medical narratives in comics, Williams set up the *Graphic Medicine* website as a hub for clinicians and scholars. This does not only mean medical memoir and illness narratives from the patient's perspective (though this makes up a large percentage of texts), but also narratives from the point of view of clinicians or medical researchers; non-fiction comics that give accessible information about a specific condition or treatment; and guides for those who are tangential to the patient experience, such as loved ones and carers. Many creators also work in healthcare. Williams is the creator of two graphic novels (*The Bad Doctor* [2010] and *The Lady Doctor* [2019]) that follow GPs working in rural Wales, their roles as doctors, and how their personal health concerns affect their work. As another example, M.K. Czerwiec (alias 'Comic Nurse') works as an HIV hospice nurse and has been recording her experiences in comics form for many years. Her work is available in book form (*Comic Nurse* [2006]) and on her website.

When it comes to the subgenre of Graphic Medicine that is explicitly autographical, we find 'cartoonists who have experienced illness [that] are telling their story not just about a wounded body but through a wounded body' (Williams, 2012: 24). The visual nature of Comics means that a med-ical condition previously described only in words can now be shown visually, leading to the development of innovative visual metaphors to represent the symptoms and experiences of a con-dition. According to Williams, this 'visual knowledge plays an important part in popular and professional understanding of medicine, yet this mode of comprehension is generally undervalued in healthcare education, which places priority on textual learning and verbal communication' (2013: 64). Comics is able to 'inform the way that illness and disease are culturally perceived' (Williams, 2013: 64). In an academic article presented as a comic, Williams discusses the importance of the 'empathic bond' between creator and reader (Figure 6.3). Graphic Medicine creates narratives of the *experience* of a condition, rather than just its symptoms and 'clinical presentation', in a form that demands that the reader engage with the narrative through connection of image and word. In this way, Graphic Medicine is both effective as a means of information transmission and also affective, seeking to make the reader feel something of the author's experience and thus empathise with it.

What kinds of visual metaphors are being used in the representation of medical conditions? In *Epileptic* (1996–2003, in English 2005), David B. tells the story of his brother Jean-Christophe's

Figure 6.3 'Empathic Bonds' by Ian Williams (2011).

diagnosis of Epilepsy and the upheaval this caused in his family, as their parents search out treatments and cures for the condition. The original title of the book is *L'Ascension du Haut Mal*, which roughly translates to 'The Rise of High Evil', referring to both an archaic term for Epilepsy and to Jean-Christophe's *grand mal* seizures. The direct focus of the narrative is not Jean-Christophe himself. If anything, he is a minor player in a story that centres on his health. Rather, the main character is a young David (here called by his childhood nickname 'Fafou') and his rich, obsessive imagination. For Fafou, his imagination becomes a suit of armour he can put on to protect himself from the events surrounding him. The art within the book shows childlike dreams of battles and monsters, with his brother's Epilepsy represented as a snake with a crocodile's head and an endless body and with Fafou buffered against the onslaught of the disease by his grandfather, who is depicted as an ibis. The coming together of mythology, war, and childlike imagination is both terrifying and completely understandable. Looking through the eyes of a young narrator, the reader is able to see why such coping mechanisms would be necessary but can also read deeper into the images to see what the 'monster' of Epilepsy is doing to the family dynamic, the brothers' relationship, and the brothers as individuals. On completion of *Epileptic*, the reader may not be any more knowledgeable on the mechanics of the condition but is likely to have a greater understanding of the social and familial dimension. This is the general aim of autographics within Graphic Medicine: not textbook but understanding – a sense of the condition or disease and the impact it has on the patient and those around them.

The author avatar

The word 'avatar' comes from Hinduism; it is the name given to the 'earthly' form of a deity (e.g., the avatar of Ganesh is depicted with the head of an elephant). The word is likely more recognisable to non-Hindu readers as referring to the symbol, image, or name used by a person during online interactions, or as a playable character in video games. Within Comics (specifically autographics), the author avatar is the name given to the artistic representation of the author within the text. James Hall notes that the inclusion of self-portraits in paintings has a long-standing tradition in visual art as both a way to signify authorship and a way to provide an artwork with a visual signature (2014); literary and textual inclusion can be traced back throughout history, with notable examples including the author of *The Revelation of St John in the New Testament* (who describes his visions first-hand [c. 95 CE]) and Dante's self-insertion into *The Commedia* (1320). The inclusion of a version of oneself in a piece of artwork is by no means something confined solely to Comics. That said, it is something that has a distinct place within Comics, as Moritz Fink writes:

> With the emergence of comics as a form of popular enter-tainment, questions of authorship have come to meet the logics of consumer culture. The producers of comics have always fostered the notion of the 'original artist' in an attempt to set themselves apart from models of anonymously produced mass culture. Although they are the products of assembly-line-type collaborative processes, Superman as well as Batman were initially marketed partly through the labels of their creators.

> (2018: 268)

In order to remain distinct from mass-produced work, seem-ingly unclaimed by any artist, some artists explicitly labelled their work with their own name, similar to the way painters sign their paintings. Though this is not strictly an avatar, it is the beginning of the visual and indistinguishable mark of the creator on a comic book or character, something that became far more common with the rise of underground 'comix' in the 1970s. Charles Hatfield suggests that author avatars 'confer an illusion of objectivity' (2005: 115). The presence of the creator within the text, typic-ally guiding the reader and central to the narrative, would logic-ally suggest some level of objectivity. In creating their avatar, the artist 'objectified him or herself […] achieving at once intimacy and critical distance' (Hatfield, 2005: 115). We must remember, of course, that autographics faces similar issues to all life writing in that there is a necessary muddying of the waters between fact and fiction for the purposes of narrative creation. Referring to avatars as 'I-cons', Michael Chaney sees their position as 'visual figures scarcely different from any other represented object [...] on view, being viewed rather than revealing the view' (2017: 23–24). Thus, the inclusion of the artist's avatar is not necessarily about a mark of objectivity within the text as much as about the artist's own understanding of their place within the story and their representational judgment of it.

The author avatar is the representation of the author within the text. This is not to say that the avatar will be a photorealistic image, clearly recognisable as the author, nor that the avatar will even bear the same name. Let us work through these issues in sequence: first, the creation of a visual avatar; next, the other options available visually; finally, the choice to name the avatar character. According to El Refaie, 'the requirement to produce multiple drawn versions of one's self necessarily involves an intense engagement with embodied aspects of identity, as well as with the sociocultural models underpinning body image' (2012: 4). The artist must decide how to render themselves within their work, making decisions that may affect the way the work is received and the positioning of the author avatar within the world of the story. An example of this can be found in Marjane Satrapi's *Persepolis*. Satrapi's style is reminiscent of Persian miniatures and expressionist woodcuts, stark black-and-white line drawings with very little fine detail. Her style has become instantly recognisable, some may say iconic, but it does pose a problem for distinguishing one character from others. The problem is made more so by the topic of the comic's first chapter: Satrapi recounts the introduction of the hijab to her school and so all of her friends are drawn as identically veiled little girls. She is able to

[D]istinguish [herself] by the inclusion of a beauty mark to the side of her nose. This way, through changes in hairstyles or in scenes where she wears a hijab that may make her indistinguishable from other similarly clad women, the reader can still identify the story's protagonist.

(Kunka, 2017: 64)

Thus, her artistic choices both capture the central theme of the book (the veiling of women in post-revolution Iran) and, simultaneously, keep her avatar recognisable. Just as Satrapi's woodcut style and beauty mark have become easily recognisable markers for her works, so too do the avatar choices of other autographics creators; their reasons for their choices are mixed. Joe Sacco, whose work is discussed in Chapter 5, draws himself with cartoonish, blank-lensed glasses. Wendy Kozol sees his blank glasses as indicative of his status as an avatar (2012: 167); however, Sacco admits that, while 'it is deliberate now, it certainly wasn't in the beginning. If you look at the first few pages of *Palestine*, you'll see that I didn't used to be able to draw at all!' (Sacco, in Cooke, 2009: n.p.).

Author avatars are central to the experience of reading autographics, regardless of their style of presentation. It is important to remember, as Daniel Stein points out, that the avatar is not a real person. The avatar may be representative of the author, but it is still a mediated representation and not the unvarnished truth. The self that is drawn within the avatar is the self that the author wishes to put forward. This is governed by a number of factors, including the narrative itself; changes may be made to the character of the author if it behoves the narrative's comprehension and coherence. Stein uses the example of the avatar 'R. Crumb' in Robert Crumb's various confessional comics. The self-insertion is a narrative 'gesture'; the author avatar is an element within the creative arsenal that speaks to the possibilities within the Comics form (Stein, 2009: 212–213). It would be too crude to say that Crumb inserts himself 'because he can' but the suggestion that Stein makes is that we must be careful in reading too much into author avatars. Readers should always be wary of a first-person narrator, as they are unreliable to a high degree. While we should not necessarily distrust all author avatars within autographics, readers should place their trust carefully. This follows for autographics, wherein we have the added visual dimension: not only do we ask, 'why are they writing themselves this way?' but also 'why are they drawing themselves in this way?'

Of course, there are more ways to represent oneself than *just* as a drawn human. Zoomorphic and non-human avatars are occasionally employed in autographics in order to create a visual shift or to extend the visual metaphor beyond the human sphere. Notable examples include the cat and mouse characters in Art Spiegelman's *Maus* (1991), James Kochalka's buck-toothed not-quite-human in *American Elf* (1998–2012), and Lewis Trondheim's bird-headed self in *The Nimrod* (1998–present). By 'visual shift', the inclusion of a non-human avatar can be jarring. In a narrative in which all other characters are visually human, presenting the protagonist as something 'other' makes them stand out and draws attention to their difference. This difference may be literal (e.g., a physical disability or demarcation) or it may be perceived by the protagonist. Alternatively, if all characters are rendered as non-humans, this may extend the theme of the text into such visual metaphors. For example, Cece Bell's *El Deafo* (2014) chronicles her deafness and use of a hearing aid since childhood. Because of the technology involved in her hearing aid, Bell sometimes hears private conversations between her teachers; she develops a secret superhero identity, 'El Deafo'. All the characters are drawn as rabbits. When asked about her choices in an interview, Bell stated, 'What are bunnies known for? Big ears; excellent hearing': the visual metaphor continues the theme of deafness and hearing (Bell in Bircher, 2015: n.p.).

The use of zoomorphic or non-human avatars is challenging: Kunka asks if 'the value of the allegorical representation overcome[s] any questions that the representations might raise with regards to documentary truth' (2017: 64). It goes without saying that the reader knows that the authors are not actually animals and that their animal avatar is an artistic decision. However, the issue of documentary truth can go both ways in this case. On the one hand, the animal avatar makes clear the fictional parts of the narrative, which are present by the very nature of life writing but are often obscured or ignored by the reader. Although it is highly likely that the reader is aware of the fictive dimension to all life writing, such a stark reminder of this may not be entirely comfortable or welcome. On the other hand, it creates a level of artistic distance between the narrative and the creator. Viewing oneself through a different lens (e.g., as a bird-headed human, as Trondheim does) can allow for a level of critical distance that may not be present in a narrative led by a more photorealistic avatar. This not only leads to a potentially different, vital take on a personal issue but can also help the reader to empathise as they are not being asked to identify with a specific individual but an animal or other non-human.

Finally, I turn to the issue of naming the avatar character. In many cases, the avatar is named for the creator, as we might expect. But this is not always the case. In *Binky Brown Meets the Holy Virgin Mary* (1972), Justin Green draws himself as Binky, a young man struggling with Obsessive Compulsive Disorder and Catholicism. Binky had previously appeared as an avatar for Green in 'Confessions of a Schoolboy' (1968). Green states that, 'the creation of Binky Brown was one phase in my spiritual development [...] It's a slow process' (Green, qtd in Manning, 2010: n.p.). My second example also concerns a narrative of a traumatic childhood. Phoebe Gloeckner's (semi)autographical rendering of her childhood first appears in *A Child's Life and Other Stories* (1998); *The Diary of a Teenage Girl* was published as a graphic novel in 2002. Her work tells the story of Minnie Goetze, living in 1970s San Francisco, with her mother; Minnie recounts losing her virginity to her mother's boyfriend and her subsequent sexual encounters. Though the character is not explicitly supposed to be Gloeckner, their childhoods are almost identical, and she has 'a tendency to shift arbitrarily between referring to "Minnie" and "me"' in interviews (Orenstein, 2001: 28). As these examples demonstrate, the decision not to name the avatar character directly after the creator does not affect a comic's status as autographics. It is likely nothing at all to do with disguising identities for the reader and is instead a necessary type of psychological distancing for the creator. Still, as with the use of zoomorphic and non-human avatars, some readers may feel that the lack of naming parity suggests a lack of truth.

As I have already stated, autographics is, at its heart, about connection. It is about the author finding a way to understand and tell their story within the context of the wider world and in a form that makes sense. The myriad artistic and representational strategies in use may include those that blur the lines between objective truth and fictionality and ask the reader to question the text's veracity; often, this is necessary in the artist's recreation of the essence of an experience. This is especially true of traumatic memories, where the 'truth' may be uncommunicable or unreachable, even to the artist. Rather than recreate the minutiae of an event or experience, the artist will work to mimic some small part of the traumatic experience in a form that is communicable to the reader.

I conclude this chapter with three case studies. Each study discusses a different example of the connections that are being made within autographics and the different representational strategies at play. The three comics discussed are tied together by their mutual themes of trauma, memory, and identity construction. They are all also works by (cis) women, writing about their own experiences. In her 2010 book *Graphic Women*, Hillary Chute discusses the marginalisation of female artists and relates it to the silencing of narratives of trauma. She suggests that the gendered suspicion of memoir, and especially the 'extreme' or 'oversharing' memoirs of women, in combination with the visual register, are central causes to this marginalisation; the visual register is often seen as 'excessive' (Chute, 2010: 5). In Chapter 2, I discussed Aline Kominsky-Crumb and her relationship to both the feminist collective *Wimmin's Comix* and fellow artist Robert Crumb. She is a good example of the seeming 'excess' of women's life narratives: 'Her underwhelming reception contrasts markedly to that of her husband, cartoonist Robert Crumb, who has been canonized exactly for writing the darker side of (his own) tortured male sexuality' (Chute, 2010: 31). Women's trauma narratives are considered extreme regardless of their exact content; men's narratives are not, and the reasons for this difference in perception are rarely questioned. The three comics I present here as my case studies each focuses on addressing a different type of connection: between artist and the past, artist and the world, and artist and the creative process. This is not to say that each text considers *only* the specific type of connection that I am highlighting in them, but that it is the prevalent theme and forms the basis of the work.

Three case studies: connecting with...

In 2018, German-born artist Nora Krug published *Heimat: A German Family Album*, a comic that asks difficult questions about her family's involvement in the Second World War. Interestingly, the book has been published under three titles: earlier, I gave the British title, but the original German is *Heimat: Ein deutsches Familienalbum*, whereas in the US the book was titled *Belonging: A German Reckons with History and Home.* The word *heimat* has no literal English translation that would faithfully capture all aspects and so the decision to keep it in the British release title speaks to this untranslatability. Krug was born in 1977, and as such, '[t]he task of *Vergangenheitsbewältigung* [struggle to overcome the negatives of the past], of coming to terms with the National Socialist era, is in Germany mainly associated with the literature and films of Krug's parents' generation' (Grujić and Schaum, 2019: 196). The task undertaken by Krug, to discover and reconcile her family's involvement in the atrocities of the Nazi regime, is therefore not one that might necessarily be expected of her generation. In her struggle to overcome the negatives of the past, she must become acutely aware of the chance that her discoveries give her an insight into her family that is not palatable: the answers she receives may not be the ones she wants. And this is the crux of Krug's book. She is seeking to connect with the past, to reconcile herself to it, and to understand how such events and decisions affect her experience of living in the twenty-first century, her national and cultural identity, and her future.

In order to form this connection, Krug researches her family through archives, personal notebooks belonging to her uncle, and family photographs. She becomes a collector of what she calls 'things German', a selection of trinkets and ephemera that she buys from flea markets 'because [her] own family never left [her]

any of those things' (Krug, qtd in Reyes, 2018: 14). Grujić and
Schaum consider her to be a 'memory archivist', and much of
the book's images are photographs of the objects she is collecting,
alongside photographs of places and people, as well as simple
drawings of people (2019: 201). In an interview, Krug has stated:

> I think we all need to recognize ourselves as carriers of our
> country's past. We can't pretend that we exist in a vacuum.
> We carry the memory of wars and political events, and these
> memories are passed from generation to generation. We have
> a responsibility to watch what we do with these memories.
> We have to be able to learn from these things and apply them
> to the present.
>
> (Krug, qtd in Reyes, 2018: 15)

Her connection with her past – and the past of her country – is
intensely important for her present and future. This is where the
issue of the word *heimat* becomes relevant once more. It is a word
without accurate English translation and speaks of a national and
cultural belonging and a tie to a 'homeland' that goes beyond
nationality. For a country in which nationalism and national
pride are bound up with shame, *heimat* itself is contentious, and
being able to view their connection to their history and their
homeland without shame is a task that many will never achieve.
Krug's mission is to seek what is lost and to regain her connection
to her roots and her past in a way that neither excuses nor vilifies.
In bringing together the visual and textual histories of her family,
Krug creates a comic that represents many of the contradictions
and traumas of the past in close physical-visual proximity; she
allows them to exist concomitantly, and the visual placement acts
as comment. It is for the reader to see the relationality between
the different elements and to work with Krug as she pieces
together the narrative. The 'working through', to use a psycho-
analytical term, that goes on is performed by the reader and protagonist together. The connection with the past is made manifest
in the connection between reader and writer.

While Krug's book forces her to ask difficult questions about
a past of which she was not a part, Una's 2015 book *Becoming*

Unbecoming places its focus on a past that very much belongs to the artist. Thus, her book is not necessarily about the past as much as the past is 'about the book', lurking as a kind of haunting figure. As such, I see *Becoming Unbecoming* as being about the artist's connection with her understanding and conception of herself, tracking the ways this connection changes from the 1970s to the 2010s. Beginning in 1977, when she was twelve and living with her family in Yorkshire, Una chronicles her early teen years in relation to the unfolding 'Yorkshire Ripper' investigation. The Yorkshire Ripper, Peter Sutcliffe, killed thirteen women and seriously injured nine others in the late 1970s, before being arrested in 1980; the case was poorly handled by the police and led to reform within homicide policing procedures nationally. *Becoming Unbecoming* is intensely concerned with what it is to grow and develop as a young woman in an era where each woman feels stalked and threatened by an unknown sexual predator. Rita Jacobs writes that, 'in [the context of the book], the Ripper's sensational crime is seen as less of an aberration than we might expect, though it is writ larger. In fact, the everyday crimes of men against girls and women appear to be legion' (2017: 91). Una is attempting to grow up in a world that is against what she is and what she is becoming.

The opening page of the book shows a stooped and exhausted Una carrying an empty speech bubble over her shoulder like a sack; the weight of wordlessness and an inability to speak appears to be incredibly heavy for her, and this initial image crystallises the themes of the book (Figure 6.4). The motifs of a hunched Una carrying a load in the form of empty speech bubbles recur throughout the comic. It becomes clear to the reader that the immense weight of silence on Una derives from the sexual abuse that she suffers as a young woman, and which remains unspoken. Within the comic itself, Una does not contain her own speech within bubbles and her child avatar remains silent. Rather, her words are uncontained by bubbles or caption boxes on the page, instead being shown as free-floating text. This is, in part, to emphasise that she is narrating the events on the page (which happened in the past) in the present, as an adult; it also provides a stark contrast to the empty containers. Where previously she was

Figure 6.4 Becoming Unbecoming (p. 7). Reproduced with the permission of Myriad Editions (www.myriadeditions.com) © Una 2017.

unable to speak and, we infer, had no hope of being heard, now she is able to speak about herself and her experiences freely. In this sense, the whole book is a speech bubble, a declaration of self.

Much of Una's struggle to find and learn herself is a struggle to find words; given that trauma is generally discussed in terms of its 'unspeakability', this is possibly to be expected. There are myriad ways that Comics can represent traumatic experience through artistic choices, including fragmented panels, use of muted (or excessively vibrant) colour, image montages, and a total removal of all words. Nancy Pedri suggests that in *Becoming Unbecoming*, it is the use of absent or unusual panels that most clearly convey 'Una's impossibility of reaching a coherent and determinable understanding of sexual violence, public and private responses to sexual violence, and the impact of sexual violence on understandings of self' (2018: 308). However, despite its traumatic subject matter and the horrible, life-altering events discussed,

> [T]he text does not offer a story of permanent victimhood. Rather, it boldly speaks back to the misogynistic social, legal and political structures and attitudes that attempt to silence women and girls and tacitly endorse gender and sexual discrimination and prejudice.
>
> (Appleton and Mallan, 2018: 49)

It is in this connection to the darker experiences of womanhood and in her weaponising of her story to combat them that Una becomes herself.

The boldest and most compelling hint at Una's desire for connection with selfhood is found in her chosen *nom de plume* and the name she gives her avatar: 'Una, meaning one. One life... one of many' (2015: 10). Despite this name, which suggests connection and wholeness, there are two Unas for the majority of the book: the narrator and the visual subject. As Appleton and Mallan write,

> The function of the narrator—Una—is to explain the contexts that impacted on her life as well as to make sense of a traumatic experience – rape and sexual abuse – that she and many children and women have suffered. [...] In contrast to the adult narrator, young Una, the visual subject, barely speaks while fragments of her life – childhood, adolescence and adulthood – are narrated.
>
> (2018: 51)

It is only in the final few pages of the book, in which we see the adult Una and her new life, with wings fully functional, that the two Unas become one. She moves home, renames herself as 'Una', attends university and marries; a double page presents her new life, which is witnessed from a distance, 'showing a family with their backs to readers' (2018: 62). Pedri writes that Una is unable to understand the impact of sexual violence on the self, as quoted above, but this is not strictly true; though she obviously struggles with the traumata of her younger years, her art has given her voice and the story within the book is a step towards understanding. French philosopher Simone de Beauvoir famously wrote, 'One is not born, but rather becomes, a woman': *Becoming Unbecoming* represents the becoming woman of one individual and her process of connection with herself and what 'woman' is to her (2007: 295).

For Una, the work of art is a form for self-reflection and self-acceptance. For Nicola Streeten, the first British woman to publish an autobiographical comic, it is a vehicle for considering art itself – as a process, as an object, and as a cultural issue. This is the final connection I discuss here and a key issue in autographics: the connection of the individual artist and work to the wider artistic community and the world at large. In her 2007 book, *Billy, Me and You,* Streeten chronicles her experiences following the death of her two-year-old son. It is an unusual book in many ways. The drawings are taken from Streeten's diaries of the period and they are drawn on lined paper, in scratchy, imperfect biro, with the dates from the original diary visible at the bottom of the page. Rather than each drawing being made in relation to the others, as one would for a 'typical' comic book, each one exists in its own moment. The book is then assembled from the images: there is a clear narrative through the images but rather than being a fluid creation, it still retains the clunky feeling of something that fits together awkwardly. This is not to the detriment of the book at all. Streeten is writing and drawing about raw grief and the openness and honesty that is communicated through this assembly process sits well with the subject matter.

In the 'afterword' of the main narrative, Streeten tells the reader that she started a master's degree, for which she would create a graphic novel, and here the process begins. Not only the process of creating the book but also of positioning herself and her story within the world of Comics. After grappling with her reading list (including 'phenoMENology'), Streeten attends a public roundtable on Comics (2011: n.p.). Figure 6.5 shows her sitting in the audience, listening to another woman asking about women's interaction with Comics, as well as the reactions of other

Figure 6.5 *Billy, Me and You* (n.p.) by Nicola Streeten (2011).

attendees. The other woman is Sarah Lightman, with whom Streeten founded Laydeez Do Comics in 2009. Despite Comics *not* being an andro–dominated form in reality, it can certainly appear that way to the casual observer. Nevertheless, Streeten's task is a complex one, especially as her story is bound up in narratives of motherhood (and womanhood). Indeed, her book is a bold intervention into Comics and autographics purely because of what it is, without opening the cover: it is the first work of autographics by a British woman, and the subject matter of parenting and motherhood is one that receives relatively little discussion.

Despite being a memoir of grief and loss, *Billy, Me and You* is not meant to be a cathartic enterprise for the creator. In an interview with Ian Williams, Streeten states:

> The modern usage of 'Catharsis' is derived from early psychoanalytic ideas of getting rid of traumatic events through

an emotional charge, the psychoanalyst being the conduit for this process. The idea is of cleaning out pent up trauma with the suggestion of a cure at the end. This theory becomes applied to the author rather than the audience, catharsis being understood as the therapeutic tool.

(Streeten, qtd in Williams, 2011: 357)

But to return to Aristotle's use of the word, catharsis is something for the audience, not the creator. Streeten goes on to say that many people have suggested that the creation of the book is a work of therapy: 'I did not think about the work in terms of therapy or catharsis for myself or anyone else when I began, but it's a question repeatedly asked' (2011: 357). Instead, the book is a work of art. She is creating an artefact that tells a story but is not made *because* of an outpouring of emotion; rather, it is made because she wants to tell this particular story in this particular way.

And what is the story in this book? It is about the death of her son, but beyond that, it is about the process of creating a narrative about grief. Streeten is intensely concerned with the 'how' of the work. In the first part of the book, she discusses the immediate reaction to Billy's death. Her partner, John, takes photographs of discarded objects around their flat as ways of capturing the quotidian aspects of his presence in their lives; these photographs are included in the book. Streeten does not explain his decision to do this and the lack of explanation is, in itself, explanatory. There is no way to explain why people act the way they do when grieving, and the decision to photograph their son's discarded toys is a type of memorialisation that makes sense in the moment. Furthermore, Streeten's partner is an artist. The desire to make a visual remembrance of their son through a photograph of a discarded toy truck or pair of flip-flops is no different to Streeten's own memory artefact, the book (2011: n.p.). The book itself and the process of creation contained within it demonstrate the connection of artist and process that is central to autographics. As Frederik Byrn Køhlert writes,

[I]mpervious to truth claims [through the nature of the comics form], comics autobiography allows the artist to structure the narrative to correspond to a larger, emotional truth, and to visually externalize subjectivity on the page in a way that is constitutive of selfhood while remaining true to dominant ideas of the self as fragmented and multiple.

(2015: 127)

Here is the crux of autographics. It is a distinct genre in which the creator is using their own experiences, emotions, and stories to connect to their past, their communities, their selfhood, and the wider world. The result is a rich and diverse collection of texts which allow the reader access to a broad spectrum of humanity and human experience.

Conclusion

In 2013, the Australian Department for Immigration and Border Protection launched 'Operation Sovereign Borders' (OSB). Introduced as a response to what was seen as an 'immigration crisis' of 'illegal maritime arrivals', people without visas entering Australia via boat, the campaign consisted of leaflets, posters, and a short, wordless comic. Titled 'No Way', the comic is eighteen pages long and contains no words except the stark directive 'You will not make Australia home' in Farsi and Pashto on the front page. The narrative follows a young man's journey from his home country to a detention camp on Nauru, by plane and boat. While in the camp, he remembers his home fondly, while bugs fly around him (see Figure C.1). The art style is simple, with clean lines for easy dissemination and understanding, but despite the simplicity of the art, it is obvious that the character is a person of colour, most likely from the Middle East. Almost immediately, the comic was met with outcry from other agencies of the Australian government and from around the world. Aaron Humphrey describes the comic as 'an accidental backstage glimpse inside the government's international public relations campaign to deter asylum seekers with an implied promise of misery' (2018: 458–459). It was removed from the Department for Immigration and Border Protection's website, though the operation itself is still live. As recently as 2019, the campaign was being discussed, this time by US President Donald Trump who posted a photograph of the posters on Twitter, with the caption 'These flyers depict Australia's policy on Illegal Immigration.

Figure C.1 Panel from *No Way* by the Australian Department for Immigration and Border Protection (2013).

Much can be learned!' (2019, n.p.). As has become the norm with Trump's tweets, this comment revived and intensified the discussion on immigration in Australia and beyond, with outspoken opinions on both sides.

The situation in Australia, and the universal resistance to the reception of refugees from war-torn regions of the world (but for our purposes more importantly the use of the Comics form to publicise the policies of some governments) raises some important questions about the immediacy and its international appeal. This was certainly crucial in the reception and overall effect of the 'No Way' message of Australia's immigration authorities. Elisabeth El Refaie notes that 'many of the inherent features of comics, such as the gaps between panels and the semiotic tensions between words and images, work to encourage the critical mental involvement of the audience' (2012: 206). It is in the very nature of the form construction to draw on the 'mental involvement' and, by extension, the emotions and sensitivity of the reader. In the case of the Australian example, a simple caption effectively reversed a centuries-old policy of welcoming immigrants, while at the same time offending readers who were sensitive to the racial implications of the visual representations themselves, Similarly, for Lisa Freinkel, the narrative power of 'comics' narrativity depends on what she calls the 'gappiness' of the narration. Narrative meaning leaps across visual gaps and is founded on the gutter that separates one panel from the next (2006: 251). As Thierry Groensteen observes, through the concept of braiding, the gaps innately involve levels of interpretation, invention, and narrative creation on the part of the reader, which necessarily leads to greater engagement with the work (2007: 478). Comics necessarily stir the emotions of the reader and demand a considerable amount of readerly engagement. This Australian comic was always going to receive emotional reactions, with the coming together of Comics reading styles and with a universally emotive subject matter. In addition, as Humphrey writes, the comic is a clear example of

> [H]ow drawn visual representations of marginalised groups of people can be used without the involvement or consent of those groups. [It highlights] the ways that the gaps used in comics and other forms of digital visual communication can generate reader engagement, while also eliding clear statements and obscuring both authorship and authenticity.
> (2018: 481)

Aside from being a case study in the ugly negative uses of comics, the Australian OSB comic demonstrates how an awareness of the political nature of comics and the way they are used is an important skill, especially as transmission of culturally and linguistically defined comics is now easier and faster than ever before.

Part of accepting that Comics is a fully developed narrative, and artistic form involves understanding it in relation to other media. For Henry Jenkins, contemporary media are characterised by what he calls convergence, and he uses the term 'convergence culture' to denote the coming together of new and old media forms and the way they shift and merge across platforms (2006). He writes:

> Our ties to older forms of social community are breaking down [and] our rooting in physical geography is diminishing. However, new forms of community are emerging. These new communities are defined through voluntary, temporary and tactical affiliations, are reaffirmed through common intellectual enterprises and emotional investments and are held together through the mutual production and reciprocal exchange of knowledge.
>
> (35)

Comics is central to this convergence culture and is a popular nexus of knowledge for a large number of other media forms. We can see how media franchises often centre on comics as the founding media format for the franchise. Key examples include the Marvel and DC comics and cinematic franchises, the adaptation of *Manga* into *Anime* (Japanese-language animated series), and the large number of comics-to-film adaptations as well as the resulting merchandising that they generate:

> On the one hand, convergence represents an expanding opportunity for media conglomerates, since content that succeeds in one sector can expand its market reach across other platforms. On the other hand, convergence represents a risk, since most of these media fear a fragmentation or erosion of their markets. Each time they move a viewer from, say, television to the internet, there is a risk that the consumer may not return. Convergence is also a risk for creative industries because it requires media companies to rethink old assumptions about what it means to consume media – assumptions that shape both programming and marketing decisions.
>
> (Jenkins, 2004: 37)

While convergence culture is important for the continuation of many types of media, it does not mean that they become subsumed into a homogeneous mass. The distinctions between forms remain and they continue to exist separately, even though, as Jenkins observes, the movements between media are not without risks. The most commonly discussed type of crossover for comics is with film; as Booker suggests,

> [T]the rise of the graphic novel as an identifiable format in comics publishing has been inextricably intertwined in recent years with what has been easily the most important *commercial* development in comics publishing during that period: the rise of comic book film adaptations.
>
> (2017: 160)

According to Booker,

> Graphic novels are so well suited to film adaptation that one might argue that one of the most important functions (for better or worse) of the graphic novel nowadays is to serve as a sort of experimental cultural laboratory for the film industry.
>
> (2017: 161)

However, it is crucial to remember, as Marjane Satrapi observes, that film and Comics are 'false siblings [...] They resemble one another but they're two completely different things' (2011: n.p.). She stresses the difference in terms of the active reading that comics require and passivity of film watching, as well as the fact that comics are, typically, consumed by one person at a time, whereas films often are not. She also reminds us that comics are a distinct form from films: one is not a preliminary stage in the creation of the other; this opinion arises from the fact that film storyboards resemble comics. Nevertheless, the convergence of Comics and film works in the interests of both forms. Comics creators now receive more attention because they are exposed to an increasingly wide readership, while the sheer voracity of film as a practice widens what can be adapted for the cinema.

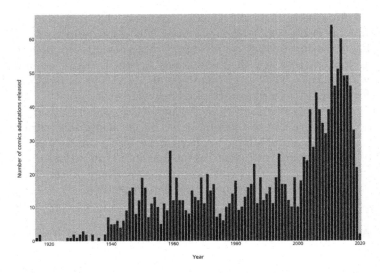

Figure C.2 Statistics on film adaptations from comics as original source.

Figure C.2 indicates the number of films released in cinemas internationally that are adapted from Comics (including graphic novels, *Manga, Bandes Dessinées,* and newspaper strips). This list was created by compiling statistics from online film information sites *The Internet Movie Database, Rotten Tomatoes,* and *The Numbers.* We can see that there has been an increase in the number of adaptations in the past fifteen years, many of which are based on the Marvel or DC comics universes. There have also been a large number of adaptations of *Manga* into feature films. The graph also shows another expansion in numbers during the 1940s, and this went hand-in-hand with the popularity of newspaper comic strips, ease of accessing intellectual property rights, and built-in fan bases that led to a spate of adaptations of strips such as *Blondie* (created by Chic Young in 1930), *Bringing Up Father* (created by George McManus in 1913), and *Joe Palooka* (created in 1930 by Ham Fisher).

The migration of Comics to the cinema has raised a number of formal issues, not the least of which is the antagonism that some film-makers have shown towards the convergence of the two forms. For example, Martin Scorsese made headlines in November 2019 when he commented that the recent glut of film adaptations of Marvel comics were 'not cinema' (Scorsese, qtd in De Semlyen, 2019: n.p.). He went on to say that

> [T]he closest I can think of them, as well-made as they are, with actors doing the best they can under the circumstances, is theme parks. It isn't the cinema of human beings trying to convey emotional, psychological experiences to another human being.
>
> (2019: n.p.)

This distinction between 'cinema' and films as 'theme parks' is not an uncommon one, though there are comics adaptations that have successfully made the transfer into film and received considerable critical acclaim. In 2013, Julie Maroh's *Bande Dessinée, Le Bleu est une Couleur Chaude* (published in English as 'Blue Is the Warmest Colour') became the first comic book adaptation to win the *Palme d'Or* at the Cannes Film Festival. Earlier, the animated adaptation of Marjane Satrapi's *Persepolis* had won the Jury Prize in 2007. Comics adaptations have appeared at the Sundance Festival, as evidenced by one noteworthy example: *A Girl Walks Home Alone at Night*, with art by Jon Conrad (2014). This comic is based on the film of the same name, which preceded it, and the script for the comic was written by the film's director, Ana Lily Amirpour. The film and the comic were released simultaneously at the festival, highlighting the symbiotic nature of the connection between narrative forms and emphasising the different roles that each played in the creation of the narrative. Even so, for the most part, American mainstream comics adaptations have not received much acknowledgement from award-giving organisations, although some have been recognised. It may be that the focus on action and visual spectacle in such films marks them as inferior, although in recent years the situation has begun to change. Two actors have won Academy Awards for playing Batman's enemy, the Joker: Heath Ledger in 2008 (Best Supporting Actor for *The Dark Knight*, to date the only posthumous Academy Award) and Joaquin Phoenix in 2020 (Best Actor for *Joker*). Both actors have been praised for emphasising the deep psychological turmoil of the character and communicating it through powerful performances. In 2018, Marvel's *Black Panther* became the first comic book adaptation to be nominated for the Best Picture Academy Award. From this evidence, it is clear that comics adaptations are proving very successful internationally and the successes of 'such films indicate a rich future for adaptations of graphic novels to film, though the ultimate impact of such adaptations on the graphic novel form itself remains to be seen' (Booker, 2017: 172).

While the comics versus film debate may well be resolved by a mutual acknowledgement of the separateness of the two forms, a debate of another kind is proving less easy to disentangle. This involves the question of whether it is possible to consider Comics as a form of 'art' with an accompanying aesthetics. To what extent should Comics be considered a separate art form with its own protocols, as opposed to being simply an offshoot of the literary narrative form? In 2005, *The Comics Reporter* published an academic debate between Charles Hatfield and Bart Beaty, which aimed to resolve this question. The two scholars considered the categorisation of Comics as either Art (Beaty's position) or Literature (Hatfield's position). Hatfield concluded by outlining the issues that the discussion raised, one of which was 'the ongoing redefinition of literary study in the face of cultural studies, particularly in light of what I take to be a re-conceptualising of the visual vis-à-vis literary texts' (Beaty and Hatfield, 2005: n.p.). It is necessary to see definitions as mutable and to reconceptualise them in the light of new information, technologies, and cultural developments. Similarly, a central concern with comics is their ephemerality and their disposability. It is argued that the lifespan of a comic is ended once it loses its immediate value for the reader. This is in contrast to 'high' art, which, according to Kunzelman, is 'immortal where the pop object, mass produced and disposable, lives a life that is nasty, short, and brutish' (2013: n.p.). However, this distinction could not be sustained and began to break down with the rise and the challenge posed by the rise of Pop Art in the 1960s; Beaty writes that 'Pop Art constituted a threat to the established hierarchies of the arts' (2012: 63). According to an article in *Art in Print*,

[T]he continuing critical view of comics as 'raw material' for real art betrays a monolithic and ahistorical conception of the medium, ignoring its aesthetic development and bypassing alternative comics altogether – the comics that could most easily be recognized as art.

(Dana, 2013: n.p.)

Thus, as Comics began to develop a history of its own, attention began to turn towards analysis of its formal properties, or what was thought of as its 'aesthetic development' where those formal properties and that development were used to align a popular form with a more durable 'art'.

It is likely that the emphasis on comics as a literary narrative form has muddied the waters of this debate, and it does not help that fan communities are vigilant in their gatekeeping and policing of the boundaries of the form (see Chapter 4). Of course, there are notable structural differences between Art and Comics as industries: the Comics industry tends to foreground accessibility and mass appeal, selling through the internet, conventions, and physical shops at (generally) affordable prices, whereas the Art world is concerned with one-of-a-kind, often extremely expensive objects that are tightly controlled in terms of creation, sale, and exposure. Ultimately, the acceptance of Comics as Art is not essential to its continued acceptance and development as a form, although this is another obstacle in the way of its acceptance as a serious endeavour.

This barrier has much in common with the high and low culture debates that are sometimes seen as being characteristic of Modernism. In his 1986 book *After the Great Divide*, Andreas Huyssen identifies 'the inherent hostility between high and low [culture]' as being a key element of Modernism (1986: viii).

According to Huyssen, the rise of Postmodernism has led to the dissolution of this hostility and produced a marked shift in the relationship between high and low (or popular) cultures. The fact that 'the categorical demand for the uncompromising segregation of high and low has lost much of its persuasive power' (Huyssen, 1986: 197) means that popular and marginalised forms are accorded an equal status in critical discourse and in academic curriculae. Comics has benefited from the removal of the boundaries between 'high' and 'low' culture, and the cultural value of comics as artefacts oscillated over time. However, the most significant single change in the evolution of Comics has been the rise of the graphic novel and, correspondingly, the growth of Comics Studies as an academic field.

In Chapters 2 and 3, I outlined the histories of Comics and their modes of circulation and demonstrated how they have undergone marked shifts from political cartoons to newspaper strips, to magazines to bound books. It is possible to see these histories as manifestations of a phenomenon informally referred to as the 'Cerebus Syndrome'. The expression is taken from Dave Sim's multi-award-winning comic series *Cerebus the Aardvark*, which ran from 1977 to 2004. Beginning as a parody of heroic fantasies such as Conan the Barbarian, the series follows Cerebus, a misanthropic aardvark. Throughout its run, it developed from simple, parodic stories and humour into a platform for Sim's personal, and often controversial, views on a range of topics from politics and the economy, to the battle of the sexes and feminism. Such views were given special prominence in Issue #186, part of the 'Mothers and Daughters' story arc, published in 1994. Through a fictional persona, Viktor Davis, Sim presented an essay that pontificated on the nature of men and women, proposing a binary split between the 'Female Void', which focused on feelings and emotions, and the 'Male Light' which focused on reason. According to Sim, male reason risked being eclipsed by the alleged void of femininity in a binary logic that insisted on the radical distinction between 'male' and 'female' identities. Although his categories were crude and were based upon long-held masculine mythologies that emphasised the superiority of masculinity, the division was taken seriously by some scholars, male and female, and even though the fashion did not last long, the debate has been re-energised more recently in relation to the controversy surrounding the issue of trans-gender and trans-sexual identities.

Sim had already acquired a reputation as a staunch critic of feminism, but the opinions voiced in Issue #186 marked him clearly as a misogynist in the minds of many readers, and the result was a sharp decline in the numbers of his readership. The Cerebus Syndrome refers to the gradual shift in tone from parodic humour and a corresponding levity to a more serious concern signalled by a much stronger, more politically charged content. A further example to support this is to be found in the changing representation of the central figure of the popular comic series *Batman*. Launched in 1939, the brightly coloured and fanciful stories of what has come to be regarded as a product of the mainstream Golden Age are strikingly different from Frank Miller's 1986 *The Dark Knight Returns* or Grant Morrison's *Arkham Asylum: A Serious House on Serious Earth* (1989). Further difference can also be seen in Adam West's camp *Batman* series and the films of the *Dark Knight Trilogy*, directed by Christopher Nolan (2005–2012). Whereas in earlier representations readers or viewers may be unaware of shifts in tone, more recent representations are much more self-conscious.

We can trace the shift in the tone of Comics throughout the world in relation to the Cerebus Syndrome. As many scholars, news outlets, and popular writers have reiterated repeatedly, comics have traditionally faced a negative press. The history of their position as cheap, ephemeral casual entertainment has proved difficult to shake. But it is possible to mobilise this igno-minious history as a strategy for increased readership by addressing the new and varied demographics of the energised readership. Comics is highly self-aware and uses audience perceptions to its advantage: if comic books are not required, by definition, to be anything other than low-level, ephemeral entertainment, then they can do anything they choose because there are no precon-ceived ideas, nor pressures. As I have written elsewhere:

> It is precisely because comics are not expected to deal with weighty subject matter that they are effective at doing so. The cultural perception of comics as a form that 'doesn't do serious' allows the form to reach a wider and more diverse audience than may be typically possible with text literature or film.
>
> (2017: 194)

The form is able to make significant statements precisely because it is not placed under pressure to do so since nobody expects to find such themes in a form often associated with childhood. As a form that can transcend educational, linguistic, cultural, and generational borders, it has proven its worth across a range of areas of public life, from medical education and public information, to language learning and reading. Comics creators have embraced their form's initial low status to encourage, educate, inform, persuade, and entertain.

Ultimately, we have a form that is able to speak, to a wide readership and in many ways. It can articulate existing myths and fantasies, but it can also be a vehicle for criticism, and its effectiveness in all these areas of public and personal life is, in large part due to its immediacy and its incisiveness. Comics is a form that can teach and entertain, while also adapting to new readerships and rapidly evolving technologies. It can reflect various social trends and the rapidly changing interests of its readers. As a form, it stands on the front lines of political, social, and historical conflicts, on battlefields both literal and ideological, and it has shown that it can react and respond quickly to situations as they arise. It can reflect on the *Zeitgeist* of the time or it can stand in opposition to it. In short, Comics is a form that is for all people and for all time.

Glossary

Adaptation An altered version of a text from one form to another – for example, from novel to comic or from comic to film. Adaptations may be very closely aligned to the source material (often referred to as a 'faithful' adaptation) or may differ greatly. Director Alain Resnais suggested that adapting a text without changing any aspect is like 'reheating a meal'; those who wish to create adaptations across narrative forms must contend with the different techniques for storytelling and representation available to them (Resnais qtd in Sheppard, 2017: 20).

Affect A feeling or sensory experience accompanying a thought or action, or occurring in response to a stimulus. Elsewhere, I have written that 'Affect is at once both delightfully simple and notoriously complex; definitions are multitudinous and theorists have long thrashed out the most effective way to explain it' (2017: 42). It is an artistic, narrative phenomenon with a long history of critical reference. Aristotle writes that affect is 'that which leads one's condition to become so transformed that his judgment is affected, and which is accompanied by pleasure and pain' (1991: 6). It is the coming together of reading and emotion in which the reader experiences a text viscerally and/or emotionally.

Autographics Comics that use the themes and techniques of life writing, combined with the comics form, to tell a true story. The term was coined by Gillian Whitlock (2006) to bring together discussions of image, text, and the self. It is an umbrella term that covers autobiographical, biographical, and memoir comics; a cognate term is 'life writing' (see entry 'life writing').

Caricature   A portrait or other artistic depiction, usually of a face, in which the characteristic features of the original are exaggerated for comedic or satirical purposes. The term derives from the Italian *caricare* (to overload or to exaggerate) and has been used in English as a noun since the 1680s.

Comics laureate   An ambassador for comic books and their potential to improve literacy, elected to the role by Comics Literacy Awareness (CLAw), founded in 2014. There have been three Laureates to date: Dave Gibbons (2015–2017), Charlie Adlard (2017–2019), and Hannah Berry (2019–2021). A new laureate will take over in February 2021.

Cosplay   A *portmanteau* of 'costume play', coined in Japan in 1984, to refer to the act of dressing up in costume, esp. as a character from comics, *Manga*, or other media forms, with an implied element of performance (Takahashi, 1983: n.p.). It derives from the long-standing tradition of 'masquerade' and the wearing of costumes for parties, pageants, and other social events. It is a popular type of fan engagement.

Cultural capital   The term was coined by French sociologist Pierre Bourdieu in his 1986 essay 'The Forms of Culture'. Bourdieu writes that

> cultural capital can exist in three forms: in the embodied state, i.e., in the form of long-lasting dispositions of the mind and body; in the objectified state, in the form of cultural goods (pictures, books, dictionaries, instruments, machines, etc.) […]; and in the institutionalized state.
>
> (1986: 242)

The concept of cultural capital collects together elements of a person including education, tastes, posture, clothing style, material belongings, and family connections that are acquired or developed through being part of a certain social class. Sharing similar forms of cultural capital with others creates a sense of collective identity that is often used to leverage social mobility. Bourdieu makes it clear that cultural capital is a source of social inequality. Certain forms are more highly valued and affect social mobility as much as income or wealth.

Dōjinshi   Sometimes transliterated as *Doujinshi*. Japanese term for self-published *Manga*. Though these are usually the work of amateurs, some professionals also self-publish. The term comes from 同人 (*dōjin* – same person) and 誌 (*shi* – a suffix meaning 'periodical publication'). *Dōjinshi* became a major phenomenon with *Manga* in the 1980s, but the first recorded examples date back to the Meiji period (c. 1874).

Doxxing   The act of publishing an individual's private information online; this may include name, address, bank information, place of employment. 'Doxxing' is short for 'documents–ing' and is typically carried out with malicious intent. It developed from the 1990s internet slang 'dropping dox' which was 'an old-school revenge tactic that emerged from hacker culture in 1990s' (Honan, 2014: n.p.).

E-readers   Also known as 'e-book reader' or 'e-book device'. A hand–held electronic device designed to be used for reading digital versions of books. E-readers typically use a type of screen technology called 'electronic paper' rather than an LCD screen, to mimic the reading experience of a printed book. The first e-reader, the 'Sony Libre', was launched in 2004. The most popular to date is the Amazon Kindle, which has sold over 20 million units since its launch in 2007 (Kozlowski, 2018: n.p.).

Ergodic literature   A term coined by Espen Aarseth in his 1997 book *Cybertext: Perspectives on Ergodic Literature*. It is derived from the Greek ἔργον (*ergon* – work) and ὁδός (*hodos* – path) and refers to literature that does not follow a clear reading path or requires a considerable amount of work on the part of the reader.

Fan fiction and art   Works of narrative or decorative art created by fans of a text, artist, or character, in order to participate in their fandom and engage with the source material. The term was first used in 1939 as a disparaging term to distinguish between science fiction novels written by amateurs and 'pro fiction', written by professional writers (Prucher, 2007: 57).

Gatekeeping   The act of controlling, and often limiting, access to a community or artefact by those within the community. The terms originally appeared in Kurt Lewin's book publication *Forces Behind Food Habits and Methods of Change* (1943). Lewin studied the processes by which families changed their food consumption during the Second World War; the 'gatekeeper' was usually the housewife. Since then, the term has developed into a, typically pejorative, description of one who seeks to protect their object/community of interest by placing a high bar for 'entry', such as possessing niche or large amounts of knowledge. 'Gatekeepers' are often heavily involved in fan activities and have a low opinion of those they consider as 'fake' fans.

Geek   A subculture of enthusiasts that is traditionally associated with low forms of media (comics, anime, science fiction, video games, etc.). The word 'geek' comes from Low German *Geck*, meaning a 'fool' or 'freak', and was often used in reference to circus performers throughout the eighteenth and nineteenth centuries (*Etymology Online*, 2020: n.p.). The word took on its modern meaning as a person 'perceived to be overly intellectual, boring, or socially awkward' in the 1970s and 1980s.

Hermeneutics   The study and understanding of textual interpretation. It is derived from the Greek word ἑρμηνεύω (*hermēneuō* – translate or interpret), which suggests a link to the messenger god, Hermes. Though it is often used in relation to biblical interpretation, the term is also used more broadly, referring to written, verbal, and non-verbal texts.

Interdisciplinarity   Work (typically academic) that brings together two or more academic, scientific, or artistic disciplines. Though we may think of interdisciplinarity as a twentieth and twenty-first century concept, this is not strictly true. Giles Gunn suggests that Greek historians and dramatists used elements from a wide range of other disciplines, including philosophy and medicine, to develop their understanding of their own fields (1992: 239–240).

Lazaretto A quarantine area for people travelling by sea, initially set up to stop the spread of Leprosy, a highly infectious disease. The name derives from the biblical parable of Lazarus and the rich man, appearing in the Gospel of St Luke (Luke 16:19–31). Lazarus is a beggar 'covered in sores', traditionally interpreted as a description of Leprosy (Luke 16:21).

Life writing A general term for a genre of storytelling that includes autobiography, biography, memoir, diaries, letters, testimonies, and blogs; it is also sometimes used to describe the collection of information relating to one's genealogy and the building of a family tree or similar record.

Modernism An artistic and literary movement that began in the late nineteenth century and ended in the 1930s. Modernists believed that the arts, faith, philosophy, and the sciences were no longer fitting for their roles and that the increasingly industrialised world demanded new ways to engages with the social, political, and economic environment. This is most clearly encapsulated in Ezra Pound's 1934 exhortation: 'Make it new!' In addition, modernists rejected the sense of certainty and epistemological security that they claimed was found in the Enlightenment thinking of the eighteenth and nineteenth centuries, preferring instead to focus on self-conscious experimentation and engagement with the self, consciousness, and the personal. Noted thinkers and artists of the modernist period include the artists Picasso, Seurat, and Matisse; poets T.S. Eliot and e.e. cummings; writers Virginia Woolf, James Joyce, and Samuel Beckett; and thinkers Henri Bergson, Walter Benjamin, and Edmund Husserl.

Onomatopoeia From the Greek ὀνοματοποιία (ὄνομα – name and ποιέω – to make), an onomatopoeia is a word that phonetically imitates the sound it describes. Examples include words such as 'crackle' or 'smash', as well as many animal noises, such as 'oink' or 'miaow'.

Paratext   The material that surrounds or supplements a published work, such as front cover, introduction, footnotes, interviews, and letters pages (common in many comics). Literary theorist Gérard Genette writes that a paratext is

> a zone between text and off-text, a zone not only of transition but also of transaction: a privileged place of pragmatics and a strategy, of an influence on the public, an influence that is at the service of a better reception for the text and a more pertinent reading of it.
>
> (1997: 2)

Plagiarism   The act of taking another's work and presenting it as one's own. The term comes from the Latin word *plagiarius* (kidnapper) and is most commonly used in academic and publishing circles to denote 'work stealing' but can also be used in relation to poor referencing and citation practices.

Postmodernism   An artistic movement that developed in the mid- to late twentieth century in philosophy, the arts, and political thought. It is most commonly defined by its rejection of grand narratives, overarching scepticism, and rejection of many of the ideologies of both Modernism and the Enlightenment. Though the name might suggest a simple relationship between Postmodernism and Modernism, this is not necessarily the case. In terms of the words themselves, the prefix 'post' is confusing. It is evident that Postmodernism identifies itself as something that is 'not modernism' but the actual meaning of the prefix is ambiguous. This ambiguity immediately signals the complexity of the relationship between the two. Various interpretations include Postmodernism as the result, aftermath, development, denial, or rejection of Modernism (Appignanesi and Garratt, 2006: 4). In his germinal essay 'Answering the Question: What Is Postmodernism?', Lyotard writes, '[Postmodernism] is undoubtedly a part of the modern' (1991: 79). He does not see Postmodernism as a separate entity at all but as something that can emerge within the modern at any time, as a natural reaction to Modernism. What is central to Lyotard's understanding of the Postmodern is that it has not broken away from the Modern (and does not necessarily desire to) but moves beyond what is 'good' and known solely for the purposes of creating new methods of representation in order to demonstrate, paradoxically, the unrepresentable.

Self-publishing   The publication of media by the author without the involvement of an established publisher; typically, the term refers to books and magazines, but can also apply to music, video, zines, or photography. Platforms such as *Createspace*, launched in 2000 and now part of the *Amazon* media corporation, specialise in self-publishing.

Social mores   The social norms that are commonly held or observed within a given society. The word derives from the Latin *mōrēs* (plural of *mōs* – manner or custom). The mores of a society determined what behaviours, speech types, and types of interaction are acceptable within that social group. The term was first used by American sociologist William Graham Sumner in his 1906 work *Folkways: A Study of the Sociological Importance of Usages, Manners, Customs, Mores, and Morals*.

Trade paperbacks (TPBs)   A type of comic book whose content was previously published in a serial format, now bound together as one work. Many trade paperbacks also contain additional material, such as an introduction, interviews with the creative team, or character sketches.

White paper   First used in the UK, this is 'an official governmental consultation paper, outlining proposals for future policy or legislation on a particular subject' (OED, 2019: n.p.). The term was first used in 1922 for the 'Churchill White Paper', a response to the 1921 Jaffa Riots.

Working through   According to historian Dominick LaCapra, 'working through' is

> an articulatory process [in which] one is able to distinguish between past and present and to recall in memory that something happened to one (or one's people) back then while realizing that one is living here and now with openings to the future.

> (2001: 22)

Further reading

Companions and general essay collections

Aldama, Frederick Luis (ed.). (2018) *Comics Studies Here and Now.* Abingdon: Routledge.

————. (2019) *The Oxford Handbook of Comic Book Studies.* Oxford: Oxford University Press.

Bramlett, Frank, Roy Cook, and Aaron Meskin. (2016) *The Routledge Companion to Comics.* Routledge: Abingdon.

Domsch, Sebastian, Dan Hassler-Forest, and Dirk Vanderbeke. (2020) *Handbook of Comics and Graphic Narratives.* Berlin: De Gruyter.

Goggin, Joyce (ed.). (2010) *The Rise and Reason of Comics and Graphic Literature: Critical Essays on the Form.* Jefferson: McFarland.

Heer, Jeet and Kent Worcester. (2009) *A Comics Studies Reader.* Jackson: University Press of Mississippi.

Stein, Daniel and Jan-Noël Thon. (2015) *From Comic Strips to Graphic Novels: Contributions to the Theory and History of Graphic Narrative.* Berlin: De Gruyter, 2015.

General works on comics

Eisner, Will. (2008a) *Comics and Sequential Art.* New York: W.W. Norton.

————. (2008b) *Graphic Storytelling and Visual Narrative.* New York: W.W. Norton.

Fingeroth, Danny. (2008) *The Rough Guide to Graphic Novels.* London: Rough Guides.

Gravett, Paul. (2013) *Comics Art.* New Haven: Yale University Press.

Groensteen, Thierry. (2007) *The System of Comics.* Jackson: University of Mississippi.

————. (2014) *Comics and Narration*. Jackson: University of Mississippi.

Kukkonen, Karin. (2013) *Studying Comics and Graphic Novels*. Hoboken: Wiley-Blackwell.

Sabin, Roger. (1993) *Adult Comics: An Introduction*. Abingdon: Taylor & Francis.

————. (1996) *Comics, Comix and Graphic Novels: A History of Comic Art*. London: Phaidon.

Wolk, Douglas. (2007) *Reading Comics: How Graphic Novels Work and What They Mean*. Cambridge: Da Capo.

Books on specific themes, national traditions, or creators

Bongco, Mila. (2014) *Reading Comics: Language, Culture, and the Concept of the Superhero in Comic Books*. Abingdon: Routledge.

Chute, Hillary. (2010) *Graphic Women: Life, Narrative and Contemporary Comics*. New York: Columbia University Press.

Denson, Shane, Christina Meyer, and Daniel Stein. (2013) *Transnational Perspectives on Graphic Narratives: Comics at the Crossroads*. London: Bloomsbury.

Earle, Harriet E.H. (2017) *Comics, Trauma, and the New Art of War*. Jackson: University of Mississippi.

Gabilliet, Jean-Paul. (2010) *Of Comics and Men: A Cultural History of American Comic Books*. Jackson: University Press of Mississippi.

Grove, Laurence. (2010) *Comics in French: The European Bande Dessinée in Context*. New York: Berghahn.

Hatfield, Charles. (2005) *Alternative Comics: An Emerging Literature*. Jackson: University Press of Mississippi.

Miller, Ann. (2007) *Reading Bande Dessinée: Critical Approaches to French-Language Comic Strip*. Intellect: Bristol.

Miller, Ann and Bart Beaty. (2014) *The French Comics Theory Reader*. Leuven: Leuven University Press.

Pizzino, Christopher. (2016) *Arresting Development: Comics at the Boundaries of Literature*. Austin: University of Texas Press.

Postema, Barbara. (2013) *Narrative Structure in Comics: Making Sense of Fragments*. Woodbridge: Boydell & Brewer.

Singer, Marc (2019). *Breaking the Frames: Populism and Prestige in Comics Studies*. Austin: University of Texas Press.

Williams, Paul and James Lyons (eds.). (2010) *The Rise of the American Comics Artist: Creators and Contexts*. Jackson: University Press of Mississippi.

Witek, Joseph. (1989) *Comic Books as History: The Narrative Art of Jack Jackson, Art Spiegelman, and Harvey Pekar.* Jackson: University Press of Mississippi.

Wright, Bradford. (2001) *Comic Book Nation: The Transformation of Youth Culture in America.* Baltimore: Johns Hopkins University Press.

Comics about comics

Madden, Matt. (2006) *99 Ways to Tell a Story: Exercises in Style.* London: Jonathan Cape.

Sousanis, Nick. (2015) *Unflattening.* Cambridge, MA: Harvard University Press.

Bibliography

Adler, John and Draper Hill. (2008) *Doomed by Cartoon: How Cartoonist Thomas Nast and the "New York Times" Brought Down Boss Tweed and His Ring of Thieves*. New York: Morgan James.

Altenberg, Tilmann and Ruth Owen. (2015) 'Comics and Translation: Introduction'. *New Readings 15*. pp. i–iv.

Alverson, Brigid. (2018) 'NYCC Insider Sessions Powered by ICv2: A Demographic Snapshot of Comics Buyers'. *Icv2.com*. Available at: https://icv2.com/articles/news/view/38709/nycc-insider-sessions-powered-icv2-a-demographic-snapshot-comics-buyers [Accessed 2 Jul. 2019].

Amnesty International. (2018) 'What Is Free Speech? One of the Most Important Human Rights Explained'. *Amnesty* International. Available at: https://www.amnesty.org.uk/free-speech-freedom-expression-human-right [Accessed 10 Jul. 2019].

Anderson, Benedict. (1983) *Imagined Communities: Reflections on the Origin and Spread of Nationalism*. London: Verso.

Anglo, Michael. (1977) *Penny Dreadfuls and Other Victorian Horrors*. London: Jupiter.

Antos, Heather. (2017) 28 July 2017. Available at: https://twitter.com/HeatherAntos/status/891004244089810945 [Accessed 8 Feb. 2020].

Appignanesi, Richard and Chris Garratt. (2006) *Introducing Postmodernism*. Cambridge: Icon.

Appleton, Catherine and Kerry Mallan. (2018) 'Filling the Silence: Giving Voice to Gender Violence in Una's Graphic Novel *Becoming Unbecoming*'. *International Research in Children's Literature 11* (1). pp. 47–64.

Aristotle. (1991) *The Art of Rhetoric*. London: Penguin.

Austin, Hailey. (2019) ' "If She Be Worthy": Performance of Female Masculinity and Toxic Geek Masculinity in Jason Aaron's *Thor: The Goddess of Thunder*'. In Sean Parson and J.L. Schatz (eds.). *Superheroes and Masculinity*. Lanham: Rowman & Littlefield. pp. 29–46.

Babb, Lawrence and Susan Wadley. (1998) *The World of Amar Chitra Katha: Media and the Transformation of Religion in South Asia*. Delhi: Motilal Banarsidass.

Bacon-Smith, Camille. (2000) *Science Fiction Culture*. Philadelphia: University of Pennsylvania Press.

Baetens, Jan and Hugo Frey. (2015) *The Graphic Novel: An Introduction*. Cambridge: Cambridge University Press.

Bake, Julika and Michaela Zöhrer. (2017) 'Telling the Stories of Others: Claims of Authenticity in Human Rights Reporting and Comics Journalism'. *Journal of Intervention and Statebuilding 11* (1). pp. 81–97.

BBC News. (2012) 'Disney Buys *Star Wars* Maker Lucasfilm from George Lucas'. Available at: www.bbc.co.uk/news/business-20146942 [Accessed 9 Jan. 2020].

———. (2018) 'New UK Comics Laureate to Harness Untapped Potential'. *BBC Online*. Available at: https://www.bbc.co.uk/news/entertainment-arts-45840811. [Accessed 17 Jun. 2019].

Beaty, Bart and Charles Hatfield. (2005) 'Let's You and Him Fight: Alternative Comics – An Emerging Literature'. Available at: www.comicsreporter.com/. [Accessed 9 Aug. 2017].

Beaty, Bart. (2012) *Comics vs Art*. Toronto: University of Toronto Press.

Beaty, Bart and Stephen Weiner. (2013) *Critical Survey of Graphic Novels*. Ipswich: Salem Press.

Bender, Hy. (1999) The Sandman Companion. New York: Vertigo.

Bircher, Katie. (2015) 'Graphic-Novel Memoirs'. *The Horn Book*. Available at: https://www.hbook.com/?detailStory=graphic-novel-memoirs [Accessed 5 Nov. 2019].

Black, Rebecca. (2007) 'Fanfiction Writing and the Construction of Space'. *E-Learning and Digital Media 4* (4). pp. 384–397.

Blackbeard, Bill. (1995) *R. F. Outcault's 'The Yellow Kid': A Centennial Celebration of the Kid Who Started the Comics*. Northampton: Kitchen Sink Press.

Booker, M. Keith. (2017) 'Graphic Novel into Film'. In Stephen Tabachnick (ed.). *The Cambridge Companion to the Graphic Novel*. Cambridge: Cambridge University Press. pp. 160–174.

Bourdieu, Pierre. (1986) 'The Forms of Capital'. In John Richardson (ed.). *The Handbook of Theory and Research for the Sociology of Education*. New York: Greenwood. pp. 241–258.

Bramlett, Frank, Roy Cook, and Aaron Meskin (eds.). (2017) *The Routledge Companion to Comics*. Abingdon: Routledge.

Brethes, Romain. (2011) 'Canular Belge à Angoulême'. *Le Point*. Available at:www.lepoint.fr/culture/canular-belge-a-angouleme-29-01-2011-1289191_3.php [Accessed 6 Oct. 2019].

Brienza, Casey. (2016) *Manga in America: Transnational Book Publishing and the Domestication of Japanese Comics*. London: Bloomsbury.

Bruner, Jerome. (1985) *Actual Minds, Possible Worlds*. Cambridge, MA: Harvard University Press.

Busse, Kristina. (2013) 'Geek Hierarchies, Boundary Policing, and the Gendering of the Good Fan'. *Participations 10* (1). pp. 73–91.

Campbell, David. (2004) 'Horrific Blindness: Images of Death in Contemporary Media'. *Journal for Cultural Research 8* (1). pp. 55–74.

Campbell, James. (2008) *Syncopations: Beats, New Yorkers, and Writers in the Dark*. Berkeley: University of California Press.

Castaldi, Simone. (2017) 'Comics in Italy and Spain'. In Frank Bramlett, Roy Cook, and Aaron Meskin (eds.). *The Routledge Companion to Comics*. Abingdon: Routledge. pp. 79–87.

Chaney, Michael. (2017) *Reading Lessons in Seeing: Mirrors, Masks, and Mazes in the Autobiographical Graphic Novel*. Jackson: University Press of Mississippi.

Chute, Hillary. (2008) 'Comics as Literature? Reading Graphic Narrative'. *PMLA 123* (2). pp. 452–465.

———. (2010) *Graphic Women: Life, Narrative and Contemporary Comics*. New York: Columbia University Press.

———. (2011) 'Comics Form and Narrating Lives'. *Profession*. pp. 107–117.

———. (2016) *Disaster Drawn: Visual Witness, Comics and Documentary Form*. Cambridge, MA: Harvard University Press.

Chute, Hillary and Marianne DeKoven. (2006) 'Graphic Narrative: Introduction'. *Modern Fiction Studies 52* (4). pp. 767–782.

Contemporary Authors Online. (2013) 'R. Crumb'. Available at: https://www.gale.com/intl/c/contemporary-authors-online [Accessed 6 Aug. 2019].

Cooke, Rachel. (2009) 'Eyeless in Gaza'. *The Guardian*. Available at: https://www.theguardian.com/books/2009/nov/22/joe-sacco-interview-rachel-cooke [Accessed 13 Aug. 2019].

Couser, G. Thomas. (1989) *Altered Egos: Authority in American Autobiography*. Oxford: Oxford University Press.

Curtis, Neal. (2019) 'Superheroes and the Mythic Imagination: Order, Agency and Politics'. *Journal of Graphic Novels and Comics*. pp. 1–15.

Dale, Brady. (2016) 'Sarah Glidden Paints Pictures of Journalists' Discomforts'. *Observer*. Available at: https://observer.com/2016/10/sarah-glidden-rolling-blackouts [Accessed 3 Sep. 2019].

Dana. (2013) 'A Visual Turn: Comics and Art after the Graphic Novel'. *Art in Print 2* (6).Available at: https://artinprint.org/article/a-visual-turn-comics-and-art-after-the-graphic-novel/ [Accessed 12 Mar. 2020].

Darville, Timothy. (2008) *The Concise Oxford Dictionary of Archaeology*. Oxford: Oxford University Press.

Dawes, Simon. (2015) 'Charlie Hebdo, Free Speech and Counter Speech'. *Sociological Research Online 20* (3). pp. 1–8.

Davis, Rocío. (2005) 'A Graphic Self: Comics as autobiography in Marjane Satrapi's Persepolis'. *Prose Studies 27* (3). pp. 264–279.

de Beauvoir, Simone. (2007) *The Second Sex*. London: Vintage.

Delisle, Guy. (2004) *Pyongyang: A Journey in North Korea*. Montreal: Drawn and Quarterly.

Der Derian, James. (1992) *Antidiplomacy: Spies, Terror, Speed, and War*. Hoboken: Wiley.

de Semlyen, Nick. (2019) 'The Irishman Week'. *Empire Online*. Available at: https://www.empireonline.com/movies/features/irishman-week-martin-scorsese-interview/ [Accessed 11 Feb. 2020].

Donovan, Hope. (2010) 'Gift versus Capitalist Economies'. In Antonia Levi, Mark McHarry, and Dru Pagliassotti (eds.). *Boys' Love Manga: Essays on the Sexual Ambiguity and Cross-Cultural Fandom of the Genre*. Durham: McFarland. pp. 11–22.

Doran, Sabine. (2013) *The Culture of Yellow: Or, The Visual Politics of Late Modernity*. London: Bloomsbury.

Douglass, Jeremy, William Huber, and Lev Manovich. (2011) 'Understanding Scanlation: How to Read One Million Fan-Translated *Manga* Pages'. *Image & Narrative 12* (1). pp. 190–227.

Drăghici, Iulia. (2015) 'Shrekspeare or Shakespeare Goes Manga'. *Romanian Economic and Business Review 9* (3). pp. 115–117.

Duffett, Mark. (2013) *Understanding Fandom: An Introduction to the Study of Media Fan Culture*. London: Bloomsbury.

Duncan, Randy and Matthew J. Smith. (2009) *The Power of Comics: History, Form and Culture*. London: Continuum.

———. (2012) *Critical Approaches to Comics: Theories and Methods.* New York: Routledge.

Earle, Harriet E.H. (2017) *Comics, Trauma, and the New Art of War.* Jackson: University Press of Mississippi.

El Refaie, Elisabeth. (2012) *Autobiographical Comics: Life Writing in Pictures.* Jackson: University Press of Mississippi.

Estlund, Kim. (2019) 'WEBTOON Illustrates Exceptional Storytelling with More Than 100 Billion Views Annually'. *Yahoo Finance.* Available at: https://finance.yahoo.com/news/webtoon-illustrates-exceptional-storytelling-more-130000216 [Accessed 2 Jul. 2019].

Fingeroth, Danny. (2008) *The Rough Guide to Graphic Novels.* London: Rough Guides.

Fink, Moritz. (2018) 'Of Maus and Gen: Author Avatars in Nonfiction Comics'. *International Journal of Comic Art 20* (1), pp. 267–296.

Fitch, Alex. (2017) 'Bumping the Lamp: An Interview with Graphic Novelist Hannah Berry'. *Studies in Comics 8* (2), pp. 227–243.

Forsdick, Charles, Laurence Grove, and Libbie McQuillan. (2005) *Francophone Bande Dessinée.* Amsterdam: Rodopi.

Freinkel, Lisa. (2006) 'Book Review of Art Spiegelman: *In the Shadow of No Towers'. Visual Communication Quarterly 13* (4). pp. 248–255.

Gabilliet, Jean-Paul. (2010) *Of Comics and Men: A Cultural History of American Comic Books.* Jackson: University Press of Mississippi.

Gardner, Jared. (2012) *Projections: Comics and the History of Twenty-First-Century Storytelling.* Stanford: Stanford University Press.

———. (2015) 'A History of the Narrative Comic Strip'. In Daniel Stein and Jan-Noël Thon (eds.). *From Comic Strips to Graphic Novels: Contributions to the Theory and History of Graphic Narrative.* Berlin: De Gruyter. pp. 241–254.

Garnett, George. (2018) 'The Bayeux Tapestry as Embroidered History'. *Bayeux Tapestry Day.* 17 June 2018, Oxford.

'Geek'. (2020) *Etymology Online.* Available at: https://www.etymonline.com/search?q=geek [Accessed 14 Jan. 2020].

Genette, Gérard. (1997) Paratexts: *Thresholds of Interpretation.* Cambridge: University of Cambridge Press.

Gilbert, Jérémie and David Keane. (2015) 'Graphic Reporting: Human Rights Violations Through the Lens of Graphic Novels'. In Thomas Giddens (ed.). *Graphic Justice: Intersections of Comics and Law.* Abington: Routledge. pp. 236–254.

Gn, Joel. (2011) 'Queer Simulation: The Practice, Performance and Pleasure of Cosplay'. *Continuum 25* (4), pp. 583–593.

Goggin, Joyce and Dan Hassler-Forest. (2010) *The Rise and Reason of Comics and Graphic Literature: Critical Essays on the Form.* Jefferson: McFarland.

Gordon, Ian. (2012) 'Culture of Consumption: Commodification through "Superman: Return to Krypton"'. In Randy Duncan and Matthew J. Smith (eds.). *Critical Approaches to Comics: Theories and Methods.* New York: Routledge. pp. 157–166.

Goulart, Ron. (2007) *Comic Book Encyclopedia.* New York: Harper Entertainment.

Gravett, Paul. (2004) *Manga: Sixty Years of Japanese Comics.* New York: Collins.

———. (2007) 'Where Is the Use of a Book without Pictures or Conversations?' *Third Text 21* (5), pp. 617–625.

———. (2013) *Comics Art.* London: Tate.

Groensteen, Thierry. (2007) *The System of Comics.* Jackson: University Press of Mississippi.

———. (2013) *Comics and Narration.* Jackson: University Press of Mississippi.

Grove, Laurence. (2010) *Comics in French: The European Bande Dessinée in Context.* Oxford: Berghahn.

———. (2016) 'Inside the Pages of the Oldest Comic in the World'. *The Conversation.* Available at: http://theconversation.com/inside-the-pages-of-the-oldest-comic-in-the-world-56225 [Accessed 25 Jul. 2019].

Grujić, Marija and Ina Schaum. (2019) 'German Postmemory and Ambivalent Home Desires: A Critical Reading of Nora Krug's (2018) Graphic Novel *Heimat: A German Family Album*'. *EthnoScripts: Zeitschrift für aktuelle ethnologische Studien 21* (1). pp. 196–212.

Gunn, Giles. (1992) 'Interdisciplinary Studies'. In Joseph Gibaldi (ed.). *Introduction to Scholarship in Modern Language and Literatures.* New York: Modern Language Association. pp. 239–261.

Hall, James. (2014) *The Self-Portrait: A Cultural History.* London: Thames & Hudson.

Hansen, Lene. (2011) 'Theorizing the Image for Security Studies: Visual Securitization and the Muhammad Cartoon Crisis'. *European Journal of International Relations 17* (1). pp. 51–74.

Harrington, C. Lee and Bielby, Denise. (1995) *Soap Fans: Pursuing Pleasure and Making Meaning in Everyday Life.* Philadelphia: Temple Press.

Hatfield, Charles. (2005) *Alternative Comics: An Emerging Literature.* Jackson: University Press of Mississippi.

Hawkeye Initiative. (2012) 'FAQs'. Available at: http://thehawkeye initiative.com/faq [Accessed 15 Sep. 2019].

Hellekson, Karen and Kristina Busse. (2014) *The Fan Fiction Studies Reader*. Iowa City: University of Iowa Press.

Hill, Draper. (1965) *Mr. Gillray: The Caricaturist, a Biography*. New York: Phaidon.

Honan, Mat. (2014) 'What Is Doxing?' *WIRED Magazine*. Available at: https://www.wired.com/2014/03/doxing/ [Accessed 14 Jan. 2020].

Humphrey, Aaron. (2018) 'Emotion and Secrecy in Australian Asylum-Seeker Comics: The Politics of Visual Style'. *International Journal of Cultural Studies 21* (5). pp. 457–485.

Huyssen, Andreas. (1986) *After the Great Divide: Modernism, Mass Culture, Postmodernism*. Bloomington: Indiana University Press.

Inge, M. Thomas. (2017) 'Origins of Early Comics and Proto-Comics'. In Frank Bramlett, Roy Cook, and Aaron Meskin (eds.). *The Routledge Companion to Comics*. Abingdon: Routledge. pp. 9–15.

Ito, Kinko. (2005) 'A History of Manga in the Context of Japanese Culture and Society'. *Journal of Popular Culture 38* (3). pp. 456–475.

Izawa, Eri. (2000) 'The Romantic, Passionate Japanese in Anime: A Look at the Hidden Japanese Soul'. In Timothy Craig (ed.). *Japan Pop! Inside the World of Japanese Popular Culture*. Armonk: M.E. Sharpe. pp. 138–153.

Jacobs, Rita. (2017) 'Becoming Unbecoming: Review'. *World Literature Today 91* (2). pp. 91–92.

Jenkins, Henry. (1992) *Textual Poachers: Television Fans and Participatory Culture*. New York: Routledge.

———. (2004) 'The Cultural Logic of Media Convergence'. *International Journal of Cultural Studies 7* (1). pp. 33–43.

———. (2006) *Convergence Culture: Where Old and New Media Collide*. New York: New York University Press.

———. (2009) *Confronting the Challenges of Participatory Culture: Media Education for the 21st Century*. Cambridge, MA: MIT Press.

Jensen, Joli. (1992) 'Fandom as Pathology: The Consequences of Characterization'. In Lisa Lewis (ed.). *The Adoring Audience: Fan Culture and Popular Media*. Abingdon: Routledge. pp. 9–29.

Johnson, Michael. (2017) 'Autobiographical Comics'. In Frank Bramlett, Roy Cook, and Aaron Meskin (eds.). *The Routledge Companion to Comics*. Abingdon: Routledge. pp. 192–200.

Kahneman, Daniel. (2012) *Thinking, Fast and Slow*. London: Penguin.

Kaindl, Klaus. (2004) 'Multimodality in the Translation of Comics'. In Eija Ventola, Cassily Charles, and Martin Kaltenbacher (eds.). *Perspectives on Multimodality*. Amsterdam: John Benjamins. pp. 173–192.

Kawai, Hayao. (1996) *The Japanese Psyche: Major Motifs in the Fairy Tales of Japan*. Woodstock: Spring.

Keener, Joe. (2015) 'Shakespeare, Manga and the Pilfering of Japan's Soft Power'. *Studies in Comics 6* (1). pp. 43–59.

Kern, Adam. (2006) *Manga from the Floating World: Comicbook Culture and the Kibyoshi of Edo Japan*. Cambridge, MA: Harvard University Press.

———. (2017) 'East Asian Comics: Intermingling Japanese *Manga* and Euro-American Comics'. In Frank Bramlett, Roy Cook, and Aaron Meskin (eds.). *The Routledge Companion to Comics*. Abingdon: Routledge. pp. 106–115.

Khordoc, Catherine. (2001) 'The Comic Book's Soundtrack'. In Robin Varnum and Christina T. Gibbons (eds.). *The Language of Comics*. Jackson: University Press of Mississippi.

Kim, Kyung Hyun and Youngmin Choe. (2014) *The Korean Popular Culture Reader*. Durham: Duke University Press.

Kinsella, Sharon. (2000) *Adult Manga*. Richmond: Curzon.

Kirchoff, Jeffrey and Mike Cook. (2019) *Perspectives on Digital Comics: Theoretical, Critical and Pedagogical Essays*. Durham: McFarland.

Kirkpatrick, Ellen. (2019) 'On [Dis]play: Outlier Resistance and the Matter of Racebending Superhero Cosplay'. *Transformative Works and Cultures 29*. pp. 1–17.

Koçak, Kenan. (2017) 'Comics Journalism: Towards a Definition'. *International Journal of Humanities and Cultural Studies 4* (3). pp. 173–199.

Kohlert, Frederik Byrn. (2015) 'Working It Through: Trauma and Autobiography in Phoebe Gloeckner's *A Child's Life* and *The Diary of a Teenage Girl*'. *South Central Review: The Journal of the South Central Modern Language Association 32* (3). pp. 124–142.

Koyama-Richard, Brigitte. (2007) *One Thousand Years of Manga*. Paris: Flammarion.

Kozlowski, Michael. (2018) 'Amazon Has Sold between 20 Million and 90 Million Kindles'. *Good e-Reader*. Available at: https://goodereader.com/blog/electronic-readers/amazon-has-sold-between-20-million-and-90-million-kindles [Accessed 14 Jan. 2020].

Kozol, Wendy. (2012) 'Complicities of Witnessing in Joe Sacco's Palestine' Elizabeth Swanson Goldberg and Alexandra Schultheis Moore (eds.). In *Theoretical Perspectives on Human Rights and Literature*. Abingdon: Routledge. pp. 165–179.

Krug, Nora. (2018) *Heimat: A German Family Album*. London: Particular Books.

Kunka, Andrew J. (2017) *Autobiographical Comics*. London: Bloomsbury.

Kunzelman, Cameron. (2013) 'Review of Bart Beaty's *Comics versus Art*'. *ImageTexT: Interdisciplinary Comics Studies* 7 (2). Available at: http://imagetext.english.ufl.edu/archives/v7_2/kunzelman/. [Accessed 1 Feb 2020].

Kunzle, David. (2007) *Father of the Comic Strip: Rodolphe Töpffer*. Jackson: University Press of Mississippi.

Kuskin, William (ed.). (2008) 'Graphia: Literary Criticism and the Graphic Novel'. *English Language Notes 46* (2). pp. 3–210.

LaCapra, Dominick. (2001) *Writing History, Writing Trauma*. Baltimore: Johns Hopkins University Press.

Lamb, Charles. (1811) 'Essay on the Genius and Character of Hogarth'. *The Reflector 2* (3). pp. 68–83.

Lamerichs, Nicolle. (2010) 'Stranger than Fiction: Fan Identity in Cosplay'. *Transformative Works and Cultures* 7, pp. 1–18.

Lefèvre, Pascal. (2017) 'Newspaper Strips'. In Frank Bramlett, Roy Cook, and Aaron Meskin (eds.). *The Routledge Companion to Comics*. Abingdon: Routledge. pp. 16–24.

Lehembre, Bernard. (2005) *Bécassine: Une Légende du Siècle*. Paris: Hachette.

Leheny, David. (2006) 'A Narrow Place to Cross Swords: "Soft Power" and the Politics of Japanese Popular Culture in East Asia'. In Peter Katzenstein and Takashi Shiraishi (eds.). *The Dynamics of East Asian Regionalism*. New York: Cornell University Press. pp. 211–236.

Lejeune, Philippe. (1989) *On Autobiography*. Minneapolis: University of Minnesota Press.

Loo, Egan. (2008) 'Yomiuri Newspaper Discusses History's First Manga'. *Anime News Network*. Available at: https://www.animenewsnetwork.com/news/2008-01-03/yomiuri-first-manga [Accessed 27 Jan. 2020].

Lopes, Paul. (2006) 'Culture and Stigma: Popular Culture and the Case of Comic Books'. *Sociological Forum 21* (3). pp. 387–414.

Lund, Martin. (2019) 'Closing the Comics-Gate: On Recognizing the Politics of Comics'. *The Middle Spaces*. Available at: https://themiddlespaces.com/2019/02/05/closing-the-comics-gate/ [Accessed 6 Jan. 2020].

Lyotard, Jean-François. (1991) *The Postmodern Condition: A Report on Knowledge*. Manchester: Manchester University Press.

MacDonald, Heidi. (2016) 'LINE Webtoon: Readership is 50% Female'. *Comicsbeat*. Available at: www.comicsbeat.com/line-webtoon-readership-is-50-female/ [Accessed 2 Jul. 2019].

MacWilliams, Mark. (2008) *Japanese Visual Culture*. New York: East Gate.

Madden, Matt. (2006) *99 Ways to Tell a Story: Exercises in Style*. London: Jonathan Cape.

Maechler, Stefan. (2001) *The Wilkomirski Affair: A Study in Biographical Truth*. Berlin: Schocken.

Manning, Shaun. (2010) 'Justin Green on Binky Brown'. *Comic Book Resources*. Available at: www.cbr.com/justin-green-on-binky-brown/ [Accessed 5 Nov. 2019].

McCarthy, Helen. (2009) *The Art of Osamu Tezuka*. Lewes: Ilex.

———. (2014) *A Brief History of Manga*. Lewes: Ilex.

McCarthy, Tom. (2006) *Tintin and the Secret of Literature*. London: Granta.

McCloud, Scott. (1994) *Understanding Comics: The Invisible Art*. New York: Harper Perennial.

———. (2000) *Reinventing Comics*. New York: Harper Perennial.

McKinney, Mark (ed.). (2011) *History and Politics in French Language Comics and Graphic Novels*. Jackson: University Press of Mississippi.

McNair, Brian. (1998) *The Sociology of Journalism*. London: Arnold.

Merino, Ana. (2003) *El Cómic Hispánico*. Madrid: Cátedra.

Meskin, Aaron and Roy Cook. (2012) *The Art of Comics: A Philosophical Approach*. Chichester: Wiley-Blackwell.

Met, Philippe. (1996) 'Of Men and Animals: Hergé's *Tintin au Congo*, a Study in Primitivism'. *Romanic Review 87* (1). pp. 131–144.

Meyer, Christina. (2015) 'Un/Taming the Beast, or Graphic Novels (Re)considered'. In Daniel Stein and Jan-Noël Thon (eds.). *From Comic Strips to Graphic Novels: Contributions to the Theory and History of Graphic Narrative*. Berlin: De Gruyter. pp. 271–300.

Miller, Ann. (2007) *Reading Bande Dessinée: Critical Approaches to the French-Language Comic Strip*. Bristol: Intellect.

Mirzoeff, Nicholas. (2008) *An Introduction to Visual Culture*. London: Routledge.

Mitchell, William John Thomas (2014) 'Afterword'. *Critical Inquiry 40* (3). pp. 255–265.

Murray, Chris. (2017) 'British Comics'. In Frank Bramlett, Roy Cook, and Aaron Meskin (eds.). *The Routledge Companion to Comics*. Abingdon: Routledge. pp. 44–52.

Nash, Eric. (2009) *Manga Kamishibai: The Art of Japanese Paper Theatre*. New York: Abrams Comicarts.

Nayar, Pramod. (2016) *The Indian Graphic Novel: Nation, History and Critique*. Abingdon: Routledge.

Nelson, Jo. (2015) *Historium*. London: Big Picture.

Oboler, Andre. (2015) 'After the Charlie Hebdo Attack: The Line between Freedom of Expression and Hate Speech'. Kantor Centre for the Study of Contemporary European Jewry Position Papers.

Ōgi, Fusami. (2004) 'Female Subjectivity and *Shōjo* (Girls) Manga: *Shōjo* in Ladies' Comics and Young Ladies' Comics'. *Journal of Popular Culture 36* (4). pp. 780–803.

O'Leary, Shannon. (2018) 'Comics Retailers Hope to Rebound in 2018'. *Publishers Weekly*. Available at: www.publishersweekly.com/pw/by-topic/industry-news/comics/article/76031-comics-retailers-hope-to-rebound-in-2018.html [Accessed 11 Sep. 2019].

Orenstein, Peggy. (2001) 'A Graphic Life'. *The New York Times*. Available at: www.nytimes.com/2001/08/05/magazine/a-graphic-life.html [Accessed 5 Nov. 2019].

Passmore, Ben. (2019) 'What's in Store for Us?' *The Comics Journal 303*. pp. 10–15.

Paulson, Ronald. (1991) *Hogarth: The Modern Moral Subject, 1697-1732*. New Brunswick: Rutgers University Press.

Pedri, Nancy. (2018) 'Breaking Out of Panels: Formal Expressions of Subjectivity in Ellen Forney's Marbles and Una's *Becoming Unbecoming*'. *Studies in Comics 9* (2). pp. 297–314.

Poll, Ryan. (2012) *Main Street and Empire: The Fictional Small Town in the Age of Globalization*. New Brunswick: Rutgers University Press.

Porcel, Pedro. (2002) *Clásicos en Jauja: La Historia del Tebeo Valenciano*. Alicante: Edicions de Ponent.

Postema, Barbara. (2013) *Narrative Structure in Comics: Making Sense of Fragments*. Rochester: RIT.

Proctor, William and Bridget Kies. (2018) 'Editors' Introduction: On Toxic Fan Practices and the New Culture Wars'. *Participations 15* (1). pp. 127–142.

Prucher, Jeff. (2007) *Brave New Words: The Oxford Dictionary of Science Fiction*. Oxford: Oxford University Press.

Pustz, Matthew. (2017) 'Comics and Fandom'. In Frank Bramlett, Roy Cook, and Aaron Meskin (eds.). *The Routledge Companion to Comics*. Abingdon: Routledge. pp. 267–274.

Reid, Curtis. (2010) 'Japanese, U.S. Manga Publishers Unite to Fight Scanlations'. *Publishers Weekly*. Available at: www.publishersweekly.com/pw/by-topic/digital/copyright/article/43437-japanese-u-s-manga-publishers-unite-to-fight-scanlations.html [Accessed 28 Jan. 2020].

Reyes, Paul. (2018) 'Nora Krug: Reckoning with the Sins of a Nation'. *Virginia Quarterly Review 94* (3). pp. 12–15.

Robinson, Andrew. (1995) *The Story of Writing*. London: Thames & Hudson.

Rogers, Mark. (2012) 'Political Economy: Manipulating Demand and "The Death of Superman"'. In Randy Duncan and Matthew J. Smith (eds.). *Critical Approaches to Comics: Theories and Methods*. New York: Routledge. pp. 145–156.

Rose, Flemming. (2005) 'Muhammeds Ansigt'. *Jyllands Posten*. Available at: https://jyllands-posten.dk/indland/ECE4769352/Muhammeds-ansigt/ [Accessed 17 Jul. 2019].

Rosenblatt, Adam and Andrea Lunsford. (2010) 'Critique, Caricature, and Compulsion in Joe Sacco's Comics Journalism'. In Paul Williams and James Lyons (eds.). *The Rise of the American Comics Artist: Creators and Contexts*. Jackson: University Press of Mississippi. pp. 68–89.

Russell, Mark James. (2012) *Pop Goes Korea: Behind the Revolution in Movies, Music, and Internet Culture*. Berkeley: Stone Bridge Press.

Sabin, Roger. (1993) *Adult Comics*. Abingdon: Routledge.

———. (1996) *Comics, Comix and Graphic Novels*. London: Phaidon.

Sacco, Joe. (2012) *Journalism*. New York: Metropolitan Books.

———. (2015) 'On Satire'. *The Guardian*. Available at: https://www.theguardian.com/world/ng-interactive/2015/jan/09/joe-sacco-on-satire-a-response-to-the-attacks [Accessed 3 Jan 2020].

Sage, Adam. (2015) 'We've Avenged Prophet, Charlie Is Dead'. *The Australian*. Available at: www.theaustralian.com.au/news/world/charlie-hebdo-attack-weve-avenged-prophet-charlie-isdead/story-fnb64oi6-1227178968201 [Accessed 10 Jul. 2019].

Salmi, Charlotta. (2016) 'Reading Footnotes: Joe Sacco and the Graphic Human Rights Narrative'. *The Journal of Postcolonial Writing 52* (4). pp. 415–427.

Sandvoss, Cornel. (2005) *Fans: The Mirror of Consumption*. Cambridge: Polity Press.

Satrapi, Marjane. (2011) 'How to film a graphic novel'. *The Guardian*. Available at: www.theguardian.com/film/2011/jun/16/how-to-film-a-graphic-novel [Accessed 13 Aug. 2019].

Scherr, Rebecca. (2013) 'Shaking Hands with Other People's Pain: Joe Sacco's *Palestine*'. *Mosaic 46* (1). pp. 19–36.

Schmid, Johannes. (2016) *Shooting Pictures, Drawing Blood: The Photographic Image in the Graphic War Memoir*. Berlin: Bachmann.

Schodt, Frederik. (1986) *Manga! Manga! The World of Japanese Comics*. Tokyo: Kodansha.

———. (1996) *Dreamland Japan: Writings on Modern Manga*. Berkeley: Stone Bridge Press.

Screech, Matthew. (2005) *Masters of the Ninth Art: Bandes Dessinées and Franco-Belgian Identity*. Liverpool: Liverpool University Press.

Shannon, Edward. (2012) 'Shameful, Impure Art: Robert Crumb's Autobiographical Comics and the Confessional Poets'. *Biography 35* (4). pp. 627–649.

Sheppard, Philippa. (2017) *Devouring Time*. Montreal: McGill-Queen's Press.

Simone, Gail. (1999) 'Women in Refrigerators – The List'. *Lby3.com*. Available at: https://lby3.com/wir/women.html [Accessed 27 May 2020].

Singer, Marc. (2019) *Breaking the Frames: Populism and Prestige in Comics Studies*. Austin: University of Texas Press.

Skinn, Dez. (2004) *Comix: The Underground Revolution*. London: Collins & Brown.

Smith, Neil (2010). 'Race Row Continues to Dog Tintin's Footsteps'. *BBC Online*. Available at: http://news.bbc.co.uk/2/hi/entertainment/arts_and_culture/8648694.stm [Accessed 17 Jun. 2019].

Smith, Sidonie. (1990) 'Construing Truth in Lying Mouths'. *Studies in the Literary Imagination 23* (2). pp. 145–164.

Smolderen, Thierry. (2014) *The Origins of Comics: From William Hogarth to Winsor McCay*. Jackson: University Press of Mississippi.

Soret, Frédéric. (1929) *Zehn Jahre bei Goethe: Erinnerungen an Weimars klassische Zeit*. Leipzig: F.A. Brockhaus.

Spiegelman, Art. (2011) *MetaMaus*. New York: Pantheon.

Springhall, John. (1999) *Youth, Popular Culture and Moral Panics*. New York: St. Martin's Press.

Spurgeon, Tom. (2016) 'The Comics Reporter Interviews Sarah Glidden'. *Drawn & Quarterly*. Available at: www.drawnandquarterly. com/press/2017/01/comics-reporter-interviews-sarah-glidden [Accessed 3 Sep. 2019].

Stein, Daniel. (2009) 'Was ist ein Comic-Autor? Autorinszenierung in autobiografischen Comics und Selbstporträts'. In Stephan Ditschke, Katerina Kroucheva, and Daniel Stein (eds.). *Comics: Zur Geschichte und Theorie eines populärkulturellen Mediums*. Bielefeld: Transcript. pp. 201–237.

Stein, Daniel and Jan-Noël Thon. (2015) *From Comic Strips to Graphic Novels: Contributions to the Theory and History of Graphic Narrative*. Berlin: De Gruyter.

Stoll, Jeremy. (2017) 'Comics in India'. In Frank Bramlett, Roy Cook, and Aaron Meskin (eds.). *The Routledge Companion to Comics*. Abingdon: Routledge. pp. 88–97.

Streeten, Nicola. (2011) *Billy, Me & You*. Brighton: Myriad Editions.

Takahashi, Nobuyuki. (1984) 'Hero Costume Operation'. *My Anime*. pp. 105–106.

Thompson, Carl. (2011) *Travel Writing*. Abingdon: Routledge.

Thompson, Harry. (1991) *Tintin: Hergé and His Creation*. London: Hodder and Stoughton.

Thorn, Matt. (2001) 'Shōjo Manga—Something for the Girls'. *The Japan Quarterly 48* (3). pp. 1–4.

Trump, Donald. (2019) 27 June 2019. Available at: https://twitter. com/realDonaldTrump/status/1144033134129758208 [Accessed 8 Feb. 2020].

Una. (2015) *Becoming Unbecoming*. Brighton: Myriad Editions.

University of Glasgow Library. (2005) 'The Glasgow Looking Glass'. *University of Glasgow Library Special Collections and Archive*. Available at: http://special.lib.gla.ac.uk/exhibns/month/june2005.html [Accessed 25 Jul. 2019].

Upton, Chris. (2006) 'The Birth of England's Pocket Cartoon'. *The Birmingham Post*. 21 Oct, 2006.

Vanderbeke, Dirk. (2010) 'In the art of the observer: graphic novels as political journalism'. In Mark Berninger, Jochen Ecke and Gideon Haberkorn (eds.). *Comics as a Nexus of Culture*. Jefferson: McFarland. pp. 70–81.

Verma, Tarishi. (2015) 'Laughing through Our Worries: The Indian Web Comics'. *Hindustan Times*. Available at: www.hindustantimes.com/ books/laughing-through-our-worries-the-indian-web-comics/ storye6RDl58hD3NGVTKiK5IF0K.html [Accessed 5 Apr. 2019].

Venuti, Lawrence. (2012) 'Introduction'. In Lawrence Venuti (ed.). *The Translation Studies Reader.* Abingdon: Routledge. pp. 1–10.

Versaci, Rocco. (2012) *This Book Contains Graphic Language: Comics as Literature.* London: Continuum.

Walker, Tristram. (2010) 'Graphic Wound: The Comics Journalism of Joe Sacco'. *Journeys 11* (1). pp. 69–88.

Watt, Ian. (2001) *The Rise of the Novel: Studies in Defoe, Richardson and Fielding.* Berkeley: University of Los Angeles.

Weber, Wibke and Hans-Martin Rall. (2017) 'Authenticity in Comics Journalism: Visual Strategies for Reporting Facts'. *Journal of Graphic Novels and Comics 8* (4). pp. 376–397.

Weida, Courtney Lee. (2011) 'Wonder(ing) Women: Investigating Gender Politics and Art Education Within Graphica'. *Visual Culture & Gender 6.* pp. 99–108.

Weissbort, Daniel and Ástráður Eysteinsson. (2006) *Translation Theory and Practice: A Historical Reader.* Oxford: Oxford University Press.

Welker, James. (2015) 'A Brief History of Shōnen'ai, Yaoi, and Boys Love'. In Mark McLelland, Kazumi Nagaike, Katsuhiko Suganuma, and James Welker (eds.). *Boys Love Manga and Beyond.* Jackson: University Press of Mississippi. pp. 42–75.

Whitlock, Gillian. (2006) 'Autographics: The Seeing "I" of Comics'. *Modern Fiction Studies 52* (4). pp. 965–979.

———. (2007) *Soft Weapons: Autobiography in Transit.* Chicago: University of Chicago Press.

Williams, Ian. (2007) 'Why Graphic Medicine?' *Graphic Medicine.* Available at: www.graphicmedicine.org/why-graphic-medicine/ [Accessed 23 Oct. 2019].

———. (2011) 'Autography as Auto-Therapy: Psychic Pain and the Graphic Memoir'. *Journal of Medical Humanities 32* (4). pp. 353–366.

———. (2012) 'Graphic Medicine: Comics as Medical Narrative'. *Medical Humanities 38* (1). pp. 21–27.

———. (2013) 'Graphic Medicine: The Portrayal of Illness in Underground and Autobiographical Comics'. In Victoria Bates, Alan Bleakley, and Sam Goodman (eds.). *Medicine, Health and the Arts: Approaches to the Medical Humanities.* London: Routledge.

———. (2014) *The Bad Doctor.* Oxford: Myriad Editions.

Williams, Kristian. (2003) 'The Case for Comics Journalism'. *Columbia Journalism Review 43* (6). pp. 51–55.

Wingfield Digby, George. (1957) 'Technique and Production'. In Frank Stenton (ed.). *The Bayeux Tapestry.* London: Phaidon. pp. 37–55.

Witek, Joseph. (2004) 'Why Art Spiegelman Doesn't Draw Comics'. *ImageTexT: Interdisciplinary Comics Studies 1* (1). Available at: http:// imagetext.english.ufl.edu/archives/v1_1/witek/#:~:text=Most%20 notable%20was%20the%20New,Spiegelman%20is%20an%20 original%2C%20a/. [Accessed 1 Feb 2020].

Wolk, Douglas. (2003) 'Please, Sir, I Want Some Moore: The lazy British Genius Who Transformed American Comics'. *Slate Magazine*. Available at: https://slate.com/culture/2003/12/how-alan-moore-transformed-american-comics.html [Accessed 24 Sep. 2019].

———. (2007) *Reading Comics: How Graphic Novels Work and What They Mean*. Cambridge: Da Capo.

Woo, Benjamin. (2010) 'Reconsidering Comics Journalism: Information and Experience in Joe Sacco's Palestine'. In Joyce Goggin and Dan Hassler-Forest (eds.). *The Rise and Reason of Comics and Graphic Literature: Critical Essays on the Form*. Durham: McFarland. pp. 166–177.

Wright, Bradford W. (2003) *Comic Book Nation: The Transformation of Youth Culture in America*. Baltimore: Johns Hopkins University Press.

Yoshihara, Yukari. (2016) 'Toward "Reciprocal Legitimation" between Shakespeare's Works and Manga'. *Multicultural Shakespeare: Translation, Appropriation and Performance 14* (29). pp 107–122.

Yoshizumi, Kyoko. (1995) 'Marriage and Family: Past and Present'. In Kumiko Fujimura-Fanselow and Atsuko Kameda (eds.). *Japanese Women: New Feminist Perspectives on the Past, Present, and Future*. New York: Feminist Press CUNY. pp. 183–197.

Zanettin, Federico. (2005) 'Comics in Translation Studies: An Overview and Suggestions for Research'. *Actas do VII Seminário de Tradução Científica e Técnica em Língua Portuguesa 2004: Tradução e Interculturalismo*. Lisbon: União Latina. pp. 93–98.

——— (ed.). (2008) *Comics in Translation*. Manchester: St Jerome.

Index